CASE STUDIES IN SPORT SOCIALISATION

Mark Brooke

CASE STUDIES IN SPORT SOCIALISATION

Mark Brooke

COMMON GROUND RESEARCH NETWORKS 2019

First published in 2019
as part of the Sport & Society Book Imprint
http://doi.org/ 10.18848/978-1-86335-144-7/CGP (Full Book)

Common Ground Research Networks
2001 South First Street, Suite 202
University of Illinois Research Park
Champaign, IL
61820

Library of Congress Cataloging-in-Publication Data

Names: Brooke, Mark, author.
Title: Case studies in sport socialisation / Mark Brooke.
Other titles: Case studies in sport socialization
Description: Champaign, IL : Common Ground Research Networks, 2019. |
    Includes bibliographical references.
Identifiers: LCCN 2018060449 (print) | LCCN 2019003632 (ebook) | ISBN
    9781863351447 (pdf) | ISBN 9781863351423 (hardback : alk. paper) | ISBN
    9781863351430 (pbk. : alk. paper)
Subjects: LCSH: Sports--Social aspects--Case studies.
Classification: LCC GV706.5 (ebook) | LCC GV706.5 .B776 2019 (print) | DDC
    306.4/83--dc23
LC record available at https://lccn.loc.gov/2018060449

Cover Photo Credit: Phillip Kalantzis-Cope

Table of Contents

PART 3: SOCIALISATION THROUGH SPORT

CHAPTER 1

Introduction

Terry Eagleton (2007), in *The Meaning of Life: A Very Short Introduction*, writes:

> 'If you were to ask what provides some meaning in life nowadays for a great many people, especially men, you could do worse than reply 'Football'. Not many of them, perhaps, would be willing to admit as much; but sport, and in Britain football in particular, stands in for all those noble causes religious faith, national sovereignty, personal honour, and ethnic identity for which, over the centuries, people have been prepared to go to their deaths. Sport involves tribal loyalties and rivalries, symbolic rituals, fabulous legends, iconic heroes, epic battles, aesthetic beauty, physical fulfilment, intellectual satisfaction, sublime spectaculars, and a profound sense of belonging. It also provides the human solidarity and physical immediacy which television does not. Without these values, a good many lives would no doubt be pretty empty. It is sport, not religion, which is now the opium of the people' (p. 30).

For Eagleton, sport is an essential social institution today; one that is replacing other residual institutions as agents of socialisation from the past, such as religious faith and ethnic identity. In the same vain, in his book, *The Rites of Men*, Burstyn (1999) wrote that 'the rituals of sport engage more people in a shared experience than any other institution or cultural activity today' (p. 3). It is true that few activities are as prevailing today as sport. Indeed, Loy and Coakley (2009), in their chapter in the *Blackwell Encyclopaedia of Sociology* define modern day sport as an 'expressive ubiquitous social phenomenon of great magnitude and complexity'. It pervades all parts of society and influences social values, social status and human relations. It therefore helps to develop a wide range of instrumental relationships that assist individuals to integrate into society. Because of this, many academics from diverse disciplines, have chosen to analyse sport to find out why this is the case. Many of these have explored the psychological, historio-sociological reasons for its growth; others have even looked at evolutionary genetics (Epstein, 2014) to explore the development of those athletes who show superiority in their sport. Reasons for the growth of sport as we know it today, probably encompass all of these elements.

INSTINCT AND PLAY

The study of socialisation is often linked to the nature versus nurture (or hereditary and environment) debate in human development. The academic discussion as Scott & Marshall (2009) state, tends to conclude that both are essential. There is an argument that sport, as a tool, enables humans to experience instinctual drives. Engrained through our need to survive, concepts such as fight, and flight belong to the functioning of the unconscious. These instinctual drives as mental forces demand an outlet. Sport's ubiquity might be explained because it is a mechanism through which these instincts can be expressed.

In the Introduction to his book *Sports in the Western World*, Baker (1988) argues that it is competition as part of our instinctive needs that has given rise to sport. According to Baker, 'where there is no contest, they create one. From deep within, and from millennia past, comes the impulse for athletic competition' (p. 1). Baker (1988) points out that in primitive times, those hunters who distinguished themselves tended to win prominence in a tribe. This has led many, among them Baker (1988), to argue that humans have an innate 'competitive impulse' (p. 3). To support this, there are still primitive tribes today such as the Arapesh in New Guinea, who refer to men who have either taken women from their territory or killed game in it, as rivals: *ano'in*. One need only to look at the Roman's Gladiatorial culture to see how deadly competition was a part of sport. Auguet (2012) shows us how Roman civilisation was a very competitive warrior state, engaged in worldwide imperial campaigns; and how this was, to a large extent, reflected in the cruelty and violence of the games. A kind of public opiate for the citizens of Ancient Rome, the games enabled them to forget the mediocrity of their condition through deadly competition.

Yet what must always be considered is that these instinctual emotions are most often felt whilst in physical or verbal communication with another. This leads us to conclude that humans may have an innate 'competitive impulse', yet, at the same time, throughout human history, collaboration has also been very present. Primitive tribes needed to work together to defend themselves and to hunt. Cave paintings demonstrate how mastodon males, who travelled alone, would be hunted by groups throwing a barrage of spears at them from a distance using an *atlatl* or spear thrower. It is highly unlikely that individual hunters were able to defeat this prey. Perhaps the bravest most effective hunter was rewarded, yet it was the whole tribe who benefited from the kill.

This is where the study of socialisation and the nurture argument comes in. Mammals, and particularly humans, are social animals. At the most basic level of communication is play. It is found in all mammalian societies and acts as part of an evolutionary stable strategy to develop relationships. Huizinga (1955) states:

> 'Play is older than culture, for culture, however inadequately defined, always presupposes human society, and animals have not waited for man to teach them their playing' (p. 1).

This is also brought up in Pinker's (1995) *The Language Instinct* and Dunbar's (1996) *Grooming, Gossip and the Evolution of Language*. Play is one of the ways young primates establish mutual trust. In humans however, the neocortex, the part of the brain involved in higher social cognition, is much larger compared to the other primates making humans more adapted to feelings of empathy. A priori, humans have a social brain (see the 'social brain hypothesis' from Dunbar, 1998, Whiten & Byrne,

1997) and as Rousseau (1992) has pointed out, many important human characteristics stem from living with others, not from any pre-social existence, if indeed, there ever has been one. This means that socialisation agents, whether primary or secondary, play a very significant role in the development of selfhood and even create what is sometimes called a generalised other, or conscience collective (Durkheim, 1957 as cited in Misztal, 2003).

Play is found in all of the widespread human languages. All of the following terms relate to play and children's games: In Greek, παιδιά; in Sanskrit, krīdati; in Chinese, wan; in Semitic languages, la'ab; and in Latin, ludus. As Frost (1992), a Vygotskian argues, 'play is the chief vehicle for the development of imagination and intelligence, language, social skills, and perceptual-motor abilities in infants and young children' (p. 48). Child play is also honoured in our literature. In Blake's (1994) 'Nurse's Song' the caregiver observed the play-exhausted children:

> *When the voices of children are heard on the green*
> *And laughing is heard on the hill,*
> *My heart is at rest within my breast*
> *And everything else is still.*

Therefore, the ubiquity of sport, a manifestation of play, might be because it caters to instincts such as competition and collaboration. It might also be because of environmental influences; the nurture side of human development and socialisation processes. Humans have instincts, but they also have a sense of morality and this, in general, has been built upon in civilisations, to guide conduct. Being a part of society constrains natural instincts and perhaps sport has this function. Many of the ancient sporting cultures point to this. Dating as far back as ancient Olympia, dragon-boating was first practised as a competitive race to end disputes between villages in Southern China. So was lacrosse; it was developed as early as 1100 AD by the Native American Iroquois people to resolve territorial disputes between tribes. Equally, the ballgame ōllamaliztli in Mesoamerican civilisations such as in Maya, served to defuse or resolve conflicts to avoid warfare. In this way, sport is also a product of the social needs of civilisation. It is a socially-constructed phenomenon and a product of socialisation.

Today, as part of the civilizing process, or socialisation through sport, we can experience *euphoric interaction* (Goffman, 1961) in a relatively safe environment. Goffman (1961) argues that sports allow us to enjoy ourselves as a part of sanctioned display of an uncertain but normally safe outcome. In other words, what has developed is a *function of disguise* (Loy and Coakley, 2009) because sports allow participants to experience emotions such as fear, anger, aggression, shock, disgust, pain, sadness and joy without the loss of life. Obstacles are constructed to challenge and test competitors' limits. However, there is no real danger the activity is a mimetic experience. This development is the topic of Norbert Elias' (2000) Über den Prozess der Zivilisation; in English, The Civilising Process. In this work, he demonstrates how socialisation through sport has been quintessential in the civilizing process. Through conscience-formation and rationalisation, instinct and impulse have been facilitated in a controlled environment.

RATIONALISATION AND PROFIT

Since the first ancient civilisations, sport may have been a controlled way to experience basic needs related to the tensions of real-life struggle without the risks. However, over-rationalisation has fundamentally changed sport. Specifically, it has subordinated the play-element at its core. This development has been continuous since the Age of Enlightenment (Huizinga, 1955). According to Huizinga (1955), play should be conducted freely without thought of profit. The result has been that sport no longer functions to enable humans to experience instinctual drives or to learn to interact socially or to enjoy play for its intrinsic worth. This is why when Sewart (1987) wrote at a time that amateur athletes were becoming less common, he saw the demise of sport. He wrote:

> 'The practice of sport is shaped and dominated by the values and instrumentalities of a market ethic. As will be shown, the idealized model of sport, along with its traditional ritualistic meanings, metaphysical aura, and skill democracy, is destroyed as sport becomes just another item to be trafficked as a commodity' (p. 173).

Similarly, Donnelly (1996) noted how professionalism and Olympism, once distinct ideologies became one hegemonic sporting culture. He pointed out that these were self-reinforcing because they marginalise other sporting cultures and form the standard of excellence. The result is Prolympism, an example of the market ethic. Thus, socialisation occurs in sport as a process to facilitate its commodification.

There has been what might be termed a dialectical development in sports simultaneously reducing its diversity but increasing its functional complexity or the way it is used in society. In the twelfth century, in Medieval Europe, the element of spontaneity was still very much present, and this meant that there was a diversity of sports. Baker (1988) points out how peasants enjoyed 'numerous types of handball, football, and stick-and-ball games' (p. 42). On Shrove Tuesday in England at this time football games were played as a final celebration before the austere Lenten period. The act of scoring was dependent on where the matches took place. In the parishes of St Peters and All Saints, the 3 miles between the villages served as the pitch. A gate was the goal at St Peters and in All Saints, it was a waterwheel. This diversity occurred all over England in this way on this day of celebrations. No game of football resembled another.

Today, in mass sport, there is much more of a 'sporting monolithic global culture' (Loy and Coakley, 2009) created due to the 'universal hegemonic trend of standardisation of sport practices'. It has become increasingly governed by standardised conditions and rules at a global level (Coakley, 2009). In this way, the sport scene that we are socialised into has a principle structure that reflects the socio-economic Capitalist system of today. According to Marx (1886) in *Das Kapital*, the concentration and centralisation of capital is an inherent characteristic of Capitalism. Marx explains:

> 'It is concentration of capitals already formed, destruction of their individual independence, expropriation of capitalist by capitalist, transformation of many small into few large capitals. Capital grows in one place to a huge mass in a single hand, because it has in another place been lost by many' (p. 686).

In a similar way, sport like global wealth has become centralised and its diversity has been subordinated so that a concentration of people follows a certain sport. Most of the global population follows a handful of sports played by the same rules at a global level. These are football (3.5 billion), cricket (2.5 billion) and field hockey (2 billion). Sports clubs are corporations and most of the profit amassed is contained within a few sports. In Market Watch (http://www.marketwatch.com/story/the-nfl-made-13-billion-last-season-see-how-it-stacks-up-against-other-leagues-2016-07-01), the top 10 sports leagues by revenue are reported. Unsurprisingly, the first five are National Football League (NFL): $13 billion; Major League Baseball (MLB): $9.5 billion; Premier League (English/Welsh football league): $5.3 billion; National Basketball Association (NBA): $4.8 billion; National Hockey League (NHL): $3.7 billion. This concentration of support for these mega-sports diminishes opportunities for other sporting cultures, particularly the more local ones. In fact, it scocialises other cultures out of society.

South East Asian games such as Chinlone (cane ball) and Sepak Takraw (kick ball) and football from ASEAN Association of Southeast Asian Nations, have a long tradition and a strong culture yet many know little of these sports and their cultures and traditions because they are not mediatised in the same way as the mega western-centric sports. Chinlone (cane-ball) is a Burmese game from the thirteenth century. Up to six athletes form a circle and without using their hands ensure the ball remains afloat. There is no direct competition and the sport is deeply associated with Buddhism. Sepak Takraw's origins are also cooperative and religious. In the Malay annals, there are references to the game from the 15th century. Football in Asean has very little commercial success compared to its European counterparts. In reality, because of socialisation processes, namely a lack of media attention and commercial investment, these sports are maintained as subordinate to the hegemon; a culture that reflects western dominance and interests.

Additionally, in accordance with principles of Capitalism, performance, profit and prestige are today the norm in the sporting context, and although athletes may find intrinsic value from their activities, extrinsic rewards are extremely influential reasons for their participation. The process of shifting from the past to the present structure was effectively theorised in James A. Crone's (1999) Toward a theory of sport. In this paper, three main independent variables drive the change to the Capitalist model of sport. These are the degree of emphasis on winning, on extrinsic rewards and the amount of bureaucratisation. He explains that an increase in extrinsic rewards causes growth on the emphasis of winning and together this two-increase bureaucratisation. From the interrelationship of these three, dependent variables emerge 'exchange relationships' (Crone, 1999, p. 7) between different stakeholders, such as owners, athletes, coaches and fans, involved in sport. These stakeholders are socialised into having expectations of each other. For example, if an owner is not sharing the profit made by the team, the players might threaten strike action. This has recently happened in Canadian and American women's football. The U.S. soccer team threatened strike action before the Rio Olympics and in December 2016, the Canadian women's national soccer team started unionizing. Women soccer athletes are paid substantially less than the men.

The dominant sport forms produced through this process of sportification belong to what Coakley (2009) refers to as the *power and performance* sport culture rather than the *pleasure and participation* sport culture. From an early age, we are socialised into appreciating these sport forms. According to Coakley (2009), these highly organised and competitive activities require participants to dominate their opponents to achieve victory. This is what Shields and Bredemeier (2010) term 'competing against the opponent' rather than 'with'. To succeed in this environment, athletes must demonstrate dedication and sacrifice and be prepared to risk their health and put up with pain. The body is machine-like (Hoberman, 2001) and viewed as the logic of technological civilisation. Nowhere is this more evident than in the Chinese elite *Juguo Tizhi* sport system, in which child athletes are socialised, and are consistently pressurised to withstand hardship and pain, as part of their training (Hong, 2004). Additionally, the *power and performance* sport culture comprise a strict hierarchical authority structure or chain of command. In most sport clubs, there is a President, Vice-President, and Treasurer; these are followed by a Club Coordinator; a Club Manager; a Club Executive Board; a Club Coach and a Council (http://www.hierarchystructure.com/sports-club-hierarchy/). Each individual or group has specific roles within this organisational structure.

What Coakley (2009) calls the *pleasure and participation* sport culture is very different. We are generally socialised into these sports to experience an ethic of enjoyment, well-being, and freedom of expression. They emphasise social connectivity and growth in relations with others. Inclusivity and cooperation are important elements of this sporting culture with an accommodation of differences in physical skill. Further, these sport forms adhere more to the original Latin meaning of competition, 'to seek together'. Some of the sport forms pertaining to the pleasure and participation sport culture also focus on developing the mind as well as the body and harmonising physical activity with the environment. Tai Chi (*tàijí* 太極, an abbreviation of *tàijí quán* 太極拳 meaning Supreme Ultimate Boxing) is referred to as an *internal* Chinese martial art practiced not only for self-defence but also mental and physical health benefits. For example, it is argued that a state of calmness or meditation is necessary to be able to practise. For that reason, some offenders are socialised through these martial arts courses as treatment for aggressive tendencies. This form of sporting culture is much more diverse than the *power and performance* model.

The contrast between these two models enables a framing of issues and to comment on a number of important topics in the field of sport socialisation. For example, in her article 'Promoting Healthy Competition Using Modified Rules and

Sports from Other Cultures' from Strategies, Phoebe Constantinou (2014) argues that the win-at-all-cost mentality linked to corporate ideology leads participants to be overly aggressive (p. 30). She terms this 'unhealthy competition' and views it as detrimental and far from the fair ethical behaviour that sport should imbibe. It is subordinating any instinctual tendency that humans might have for collaboration. Nevertheless, despite a disdain for power and performance sports, Constantinou (2014), as many others, recognises that competition based on a cooperation model could promote self-development (p. 31). However, it needs to be balanced with collaboration. This is a common view today and its ideals are manifested in organisations such as 'i9 sports'. In his article, Anderson (2013) discusses how traditional run competitive sport leads to several socio-negative impacts on youth. He then presents i9 sports as a movement of cultural opposition to this. The consumer-oriented neoliberal approach seems to point towards changes in the traditional structure by developing characteristics such as non-contact, mixed gender activity as well as rotating players and coaches on a regular basis to prevent rivalry.

STUDYING SPORT SOCIALISATION

Significant others make up the agents of socialisation in a given society. These play a determining role in defining a person's self-hood. For Cooley (1909), a significant agent should have a relatively permanent and intimate relationship with the subject to create 'a certain fusion of individualities in a certain whole, so that one's self, for many purposes at least, is the common life and purpose of the group' (p. 23). The most important are the primary agents that act on the individual at a young age. These are intimate family members and peers in and out of school. School has an important role in the socialisation process, particularly as a child reaches the teenager years (Beedie & Craig, 2010). Sporting organisations that a young individual belongs to can also have an impact. Secondary agents, such as the media, government, work environment and the neighbourhood one lives in, also play extremely important parts in shaping selfhood. Therefore, ethnic background, religion and politics can have a significant role (Beedie & Craig, 2010).

Consequently, it is evident that studies in socialisation do not solely focus on childhood and the primary agents of the family and school. Involvement in professional and amateur sports through competition, ludic activity or spectatorship is a life-long process and is connected to larger social and cultural formations than the nuclear family. These structures are recurrent patterned arrangements dominating opportunities available to individuals in society. Additionally, many believe, one of the most well-known is Jay Coakley (2009), that individuals have the capacity to define and redefine their roles in society. In this way, socialisation does not occur solely as a one-way process from institution to individual. Agency, and the capacity to make free choices is also important. The structure versus agency debate is an important one in socialisation studies. The overarching debate is the extent to which individuals have autonomy as free agents or whether their actions are controlled by social institutions. The socialisation processes are constructed as ideological apparatus.

Structure and Ideology

Scott & Marshall (2009) define Socialisation in the following way:

> 'Socialisation is the process by which we learn to become members of society, both by internalizing the norms and values of society, and also by learning to perform our social roles (as worker, friend, citizen, and so forth).'
> https://opentextbc.ca/introductiontosociology/chapter/chapter5-socialization/

In order to fully become citizens, individuals enter into relations with others who have shared and common understandings. These are manifested in *social institutions*. For Beedie and Craig (2010), social institutions promote the norms and values of the overarching society. These are embodied organised structures which commonly perform a certain function in society and this function normally requires interaction between actors. Additionally, according to Elster (1989), sanctions are a necessary feature of institutions. Thus, regulated acts or *social norms* are a constitutive element of an institution. If individuals behave in opposition to what is considered normative, they may be deemed deviant. Consequently, operating within a social institution is linked to patterns of behaviour and violation of a social norm may upset the social order. We enter into socialisation processes to understand and adhere to these rules.

The definition of norm tends to point to normative consensus and as Durkheim (as cited in Misztal, 2003) argued, that is essential for the effective functioning of society. Society is constructed and maintained through mutual agreement, and the sharing of common values through socialisation. Unity creates a collective conscience or *sui generis* reality. In other words, citizens' private desires and needs are second to those of the dominant majority. This is reiterated in the early work of Structural Functionalist theorist Talcott Parsons (1968). For example, the following regarding social action is from Parsons (1968):

> 'Actions do not take place separately, each with a separate, discrete end in relation to the situation, but in long complicated 'chains'...[and] the total complex of means-end relationships is not to be thought of as similar to a large number of parallel threads, but as a complicated web' (p.229).

Each element in society is linked. If one part fails, it will affect the others. Social change is a slow, orderly process without which society 'is no more than a pile of sand that the least jolt or the slightest puff will suffice to scatter' (Durkheim as cited in Allen, 2005, p. 136). This complex web is comprised of collective agreement and collective action. These values are taught and learned through social institutions. Further, it is necessary to impose rules and structures to maintain stability. Thus, the need for Law and Order.

Marxists such as Althusser (1971) and Bourdieu (1986) are similarly structuralists. For these Marxists, economic structures, and the rights to the means of production, are the significant driving forces of a society. The proposition is that the status quo is maintained by domination. Elites have designed and continue to design structures, such as social institutions, that are constructed to engage the majority through processes of socialisation for this purpose. Processes of socialisation are linked to the development of ideology and ideological state apparatus (ISA). Individuals' values and acts are determined by these institutions, but these reflect the elites' values and benefit the elite much more. By making people repositories of the roles and values of these institutions, the dominant group protects itself and maintains its power. It basically creates a false consciousness in which people are profoundly unconscious of the state of affairs. For example, most societies believe that private property is a natural (Locke, in West, 2003) or an acquired right (Smith, in West, 2003). However, as Marx argued, the dominion of material property is for the rich in society. Clearly, those who have little money do not benefit to the same extent from laws against theft. Despite the fact that laws protecting private property seem to better represent the wealthy, there is a clear and overtly-established set of social norms guiding behaviour in this realm. From very early on, all citizens are socialised into understanding these norms as informal rules and formal laws.

In his paper, "The Forms of Capital" (1986), Bourdieu presents how the ideology of cultural capital, in the forms of knowledge, skills and education, helps to disguise wealth. He looks at how economic capital is primary for success and how it is transformed into cultural capital or the social assets that an individual possesses (p.54). Because of this, people are socialised into perceiving wealth as cultural capital not economic capital. This accumulation of cultural capital then legitimises the power that it gives to individuals. However, without the economic capital to begin with, cultural capital is very difficult to acquire. Consider the cost of a university education today, which can help individuals develop social and economic status. In order to maintain this unfair system, ideology exists, and citizens are socialised into believing it. This leads Bourdieu (1986) to describe cultural capital as a 'weapon in the struggles of social classes' (p.50). One of the ideological structures in Capitalist societies is the myth of meritocracy constructed to make the majority profoundly believe that there is equity in society. However, this is clearly not the case. Differences in the social status of Lacrosse and hockey or basketball can be used to exemplify this.

$7,000 is reported as a Major League Lacrosse player's entry salary compared to $525,000 for Hockey League starter (CNN Money, 2017). Lacrosse today has a white middle-class demographic. Thus, social channelling does not exist as Lacrosse players take up respectable careers. In contrast, NBA, NFL and NHL all perpetuate the meritocracy myth that anyone can be successful through work hard. There is a level playing field for all members of society. In the US, in Basketball, for example, only 0.03% of high schoolers become professional. Yet, this small percentage is highly glamorised in the media.

The rags to riches narrative is a common one. It conceals that those with economic capital succeed more easily in society. As economist Robert Frank points out, the most successful are able to continue to acquire more wealth and pass this on to their families to do the same. Similarly, Althusser (1971) argued that the modern nuclear family, school and the media were the best mechanisms as socialising agents.

These are part of the ideological apparatus as they facilitate the reproduction of capitalism. Bourdieu (1986) refers to this as Cultural Reproduction.

Perhaps the biggest trend in research into sport socialisation related to structure and ideology has been in the field of gender studies. Most developed neo-liberal societies are comprised of patriarchal structures today that oppress women. One particular aspect of research in this field is how at school through sport, children are socialised into learning appropriate male and female behaviour and homophily, or same-sex networks are developed (Messner, 2002). For example, in many school cultures, the male teams are deemed more important and followed with more interest than the female teams. Further, in many mix-gender sports, there are dominant masculine norms. Ultimate is a good example of this. In ultimate, Thornton, (2004) has demonstrated how women who lay out are viewed as transgressive but are accepted as they reproduce masculine characteristics. Additionally, female players behave and dress in a masculine way to be accepted in the team. This follows what Gramsci (1971) points out:

> 'a social group may have its conception of the world, but this same group has for reasons of submission and intellectual subordination, adopted a conception which is not its own. and it affirms this conception verbally and believes itself to be following it, because this is the conception which follows in normal times. This is when the conduct is not independent and autonomous, but submissive and subordinate' (p. 327).

In Gramscian analysis, ideology is the representation of the relations between social groups in society. When one social group makes its values 'common sense'; in this case male players and men in administrative positions in ultimate; it produces a hegemonic order.

Another area of interest in sport socialisation is the media bias towards men's sports. For example, SportsCenter used 2.1% of its airtime for women's sport in 2004 and this decreased to 1.4% in 2009 (as reported in Morales, 2014). The lack of coverage creates a self-perpetuating cycle that creates a loop of low popularity. Messner (1988, p. 204) has pointed out that the 'media has a domino effect regarding women, as the advancement of many women sports has been stalled and interrupted by the lack of funding and sponsors'. Other work from feminists such as Birrell (1998) has focused on how coverage of male athletes is primarily focused on skill and performance while women athletes are often discussed with regards to their physical characteristics or non-sport-related activities such as their marital relationships with other male athletes. These differences in coverage and presentation as well as the significance of socialising agents such as sport at school make sport a *primary masculinity-validating experience* (Dubbert, 1979, p. 164). Messner (1988) writes that sport is 'a male-created homosocial cultural sphere' that provides men with a 'psychological separation from the perceived feminisation of society while also providing dramatic symbolic proof of the 'natural superiority' of men over women' (p. 200). The image of the US women's soccer victory of the 1999 World Cup against China was dominated by Brandi Chastain's photograph whilst she was on knees with her shirt off in her sports bra. This was the main cover of *Sports Illustrated* and the front pages of newspapers around the world. It seemed to be of greater significance than the victory itself. The (male) press found this outrageous, perhaps because Chastain had an athletic rather than a petite frame.

The women of countries such as Saudi Arabia are faced with powerful patriarchal structures oppressing them and socialising them out of sport. In April 2012, Saudi Arabian Olympic Committee head legislated against the participation of female athletes at the Summer Olympics in London. Saudi Arabia's refusal to send women to the Olympics went against the Olympic charter which states that 'any form of discrimination with regard to a country or a person on grounds of race, religion, politics, sex or otherwise is incompatible with belonging to the Olympic Movement'. Human Rights Watch (2016) state:

> 'Inside Saudi Arabia, widespread discrimination still hampers access to sports for Saudi women and girls, including in public education. This exists against a backdrop of pervasive discrimination that constrains women's day-to-day lives in Saudi Arabia' https://www.hrw.org/news/2016/08/04/saudi-arabia-women-are-changing-game.

In the face of this discrimination, however, recently, in the Rio Games of 2017, the first Hijabi athlete, Ibtihaj Muhammad, an American sabre fencer, stood on the medal podium. In March 2017 Nike announced the release of its *Pro Hijab*. This kind of development may help to socialise more Saudi women into sport.

Structure and Agency

With regards to the structuralists' views on the importance of socialisation through social institutions, questions regarding the role of human agency emerge. Althusser and Bourdieu posit that social institutions construct consciousness and constrain the majority's acts, dominating individual human agency. Durkheim (as cited in Allen, 2005) argues that the social facts we experience are inherited from collective agents pursuing collective, not individual goals. In both instances, these theories leave little importance to human agency. In fact, in much of the discussion around the processes of socialisation, there are conflicting theories about the relationship between structure and individual agency. Some argue that what we know, and experience of social reality is comprised of individual human agents and their social interactions. This has led Marxist activists and cultural theorists such as Gramsci (1971) and Williams (1977) to point out that individual agency can impact social institutions. For Gramsci (as cited in Strinati, 1995), power is maintained through socialisation:

> 'Hegemony operates culturally and ideologically through the institutions of civil society which characterises mature liberal-democratic, capitalist societies. These institutions include education, the family, the church, the mass media, popular culture, etc' (pp.168-169).

From a Gramscian perspective, socialisation has an instrumental role in spreading and reinforcing the dominant hegemony. This is done in a profound way. Williams (1977) states that hegemonic forces are integral to practical consciousness so much so that they 'seem to most of us the pressures and limits of common sense' (p. 110). However, through his concept of hegemony, Gramsci also attempted to recognise the importance of agency. For him, hegemony or power is a dynamic notion in constant flux as renegotiations take place between classes. Individuals define themselves through their culture or 'structures of feeling' (Williams, 1977). Ideology is constructed through the patterns of behaviour and the values inherent to the social processes of culture-making. Consequently, and in contrast to the structuralist viewpoint, not only is consciousness controlled in society by the dominant group, but it is also expressed by the dominated. Strinati (1995) points out how the subordinated groups are accepting because they have reason of their own to be so (p. 166).

This notion of different social groups renegotiating social norms has profound meaning for studies in socialisation. Social struggle creates ideas that simultaneously promote and seek to prevent pivotal change in society. This produces the long struggle of the *War of Position* (Gramsci, as cited in Strinati, 1995). It occurs across institutions. In order for transformation to be enacted, civil society is first said to require change to undermine the prevailing hegemony (Strinati, 1995, p.169). The consciousness of this need for change in the realm of ideas and behaviours leads to the subaltern groups constructs of ideology through social institutions. These tensions form an ideological battleground in society (Williams, 1977, p.108).

One good example of social groups renegotiating social norms is the skateboarding culture; others are ultimate frisbee and ultra-running. It has already been noted how Huizinga (1955) argues that the play element of sport is subordinated in a profit-driven environment. Researchers have looked at how ultimate frisbee has left behind its original values of self-refereeing, non–contact and mixed gender, also known as the 'spirit of the game', (Griggs, 2009). With the development of Prolympist ultimate, it is seen as a viable candidate for the 2024 Olympics. Skateboarding has also become the product of socialising forces and been nominated an Olympic sport recently and will be included in the Tokyo 2020 games. It is clearly now in the realm of professionalism. Gary Ream, president of Camp Woodward and the International Skateboarding Federation (ISF) has stated that the sport is all about sponsorship (as reported in Butler, 2017). Yet its origins and many of its contemporary advocates do not vindicate this change. They posit that commercialisation is detrimental to its inherent culture and anti-establishment spirit. Skating is more an expressive than an instrumental activity. For many skaters, commercialisation reduces freedom because it controls the sport by standardising it. One skater has said 'every skate park is like a cage' (cited in Beal, 2013, p. 100). This demonstrates how skaters prefer their autonomy to skate where they like.

Applying Gramsci's (1971) Hegemony Theory to understand the socialisation processes inherent to skateboarding culture, it is clear that there exists two opposing views: the capitalist hegemon limiting and normalising the sport and rewarding skaters who comply; ESPN's X-Games, with its formalised skating terrains for competitions, exemplifies this; and the counter-hegemonic, who love skating to express themselves and participate in it for other reasons apart from money. However, as the dominant culture grows in stature, skaters become socialised into accommodating its structures. We can use other key concepts from Bourdieu's work such as habitus and field to understand this. The agent is socialised in a *field*, a social environment with roles and relationships. Over time, the agent internalises the context's rules of the game to exist within that domain and constructs the expected *habitus*. Ryan Clements, a finance manager of pro-skaters is reported to have stated that his clients consider their sponsorships as 'free money' (cited in Rice, 2010). In this way, they are acting as expected in the field with some negotiation to build the habitus of the skater. This habitus might also advocate the use of weed or cannabis. For some, this is an integral part of the skaters' culture (Beale, 2013); so much so that in the Elite Daily (http://elitedaily.com/news/skateboarders-choose-weed-over-olympics/1582326/), journalist, Alec McDonald writes: '*Yep, Pro Skateboarders Might Choose Weed over Competing in the Next Olympics*'. To show how Gramsci' Hegemony Theory might help to explain the dynamics of the *War of Position*, the World Anti-Doping Agency ruled in 2017 that athletes can use cannabis out of competition. This might be a way to accommodate skating culture. This liberalisation of attitudes seems to represent a negotiation of ideas and demonstrates that the counterhegemonic group can also impact the dominant or hegemon. Thus, the habitus of WADA is also being shaped through processes of socialisation.

The sexualisation of women in eSports is another example of how Hegemony Theory can be applied today in sport socialisation studies. There is a dynamic between second and third wave feminism in eSports. Gramsci (1971) can be used to explore how subaltern groups may compete for cultural hegemony. In third wave feminism, agency is prioritised and women who are involved in cosplay are considered to be expressing their freedom to act (Scraton and Flintoff, 2013, p. 105). ESports may have been primarily developed by and for male audiences (Chess, Evans, and Baines, 2017) and there may be an inherent patriarchal ideology (Ledwith, 2009) which hyper-sexualises women portraying them with 'large breasts, tiny waists and little/scant clothing' in games (Prescott and Bogg, 2013, p. 2). However, these women are conscious of their position and empowered by their participation because men are in fact dominated by their presence. Second wave feminists, in this case, argue that cosplay is victim feminism portraying women as weak and without agency. Their existence relies on the male gaze (Hamari and Sjöblom, 2017). Third wave feminism is disempowering and counterproductive for women as it glamourises victimhood (Hamari and Sjöblom, 2017). In other words, are women socialised into acting in a certain way by men or are they socialising men into appreciating the way they behave?

The phenomenon of the hijabi woman has also developed a narrative of opposition in this way, between feminist subaltern groups. Many women argue that they are socialised into wearing the hijab by men and that it is a constraint and a symbol of male dominance. This oppression is said to start at birth from the father then the husband in exchange for obedience (de Knop et. al, 1996, p. 149). Muslim women are said to lack agency (de Knop et. al, 1996, p. 150). However, a great number of Muslim women point out that the hijab is empowering for them. They wear it for privacy, and the freedom from the male gaze that it bestows (Rozenblum, 2011). Claiming the veil discriminates 'actually further undermines their ability and their right to choose how to lead their lives and how to present themselves in public' (Human Rights Watch, 2016). This narrative seeks to socialise other women into wearing the hijab.

Agency and Interaction

The study of structure and agency and the dynamism between the two make up for a great deal of the studies in sport socialisation. The primary purpose of the interactionist and symbolic interactionist theorists is to study agency. Their studies of socialisation entail exploring how meanings are constructed in particular contexts through social relationships. Whereas structuralists tend to take on a theoretical abstract macro sociological approach, exploring social systems and large populations, interactionists focus on microsociology, the specific and the individual and social agency. As Coakley (2009) points out, individuals are conscious, self-reflexive beings who construct their identities through goal seeking and developing friendships.

There are several well-known interactionist theorists focusing more on agency than structure who can be applied in socialisation studies, in particular, the work of Ervin Goffman, George Herbert Mead (1934) and Charles Horton Cooley (1998). In Goffman's (1959) work on *The Presentation of Self in Everyday Life*, he argues that life is a theatrical performance and that we act in accordance with others' opinions and expectations of us. This led Goffman (1963) to work on processes of stigmatisation and this has been used extensively in socialisation studies. The process is outlined below:

> 'When an individual who might have been received easily in ordinary social intercourse possesses a trait that can obtrude itself upon attention and turn those of us whom he meets away from him, it breaks the claim that his other attributes have on us. He possesses a stigma, an undesired differentness from what we had anticipated' (p.2).

One stigma is the *abominations of the body*. Studies in socialisation taking an interactionist approach might look at individuals with disabilities and explore the socialising forces that devalue and exclude them because of their physical differences. The body of an athlete with a disability challenges expectation in the *Empire of the Normal* (Coakley, 2009) and produces a discourse that revolves around 'why your body is unwanted'. To illustrate this, there has been much work on media coverage of athletes with disabilities (Brittain, 2010; Yeam & Brooke, 2016; Brooke, 2018). This can also be linked to policy. For example, in the Rio 2016 Paralympic Games, the Chinese Paralympians took home a total of 239 medals, 92 more than their closest rival, Britain (Rudolph, 2016). However, shortly after the Rio 2016 Paralympics, the State Council in China issued a national action plan to encourage the abortion of fetuses found to have disabilities, aiming to effectively reduce new disabilities by 2020 (The State Council, 2016). This kind of political decision influences the socialisation experiences of athletes with disabilities and constructs their identities. In this way, from a micro-position, a study might provide insight into how individuals with disabilities live through this stigma on a daily basis.

Mead's (1934) work on Mind, Self and Society also provides a source for analytical studies on the importance of socialisation in identity construction. He (1934) writes:

> 'The self is something which has a development; it is not initially there, at birth, but arises in the process of social experience and activity, that is, develops in the given individual as a result of his relations to that process as a whole and to other individuals within that process' (p.135).

His work on role modelling is useful in analysing the influence that professional athletes can have on children. Mead explored how children pretend to be significant others when they play. In so doing, they learn expectations. For example, when children play house and pretend to be their parents, their dolls receive similar treatment to them from their parents. Older children role play being other people and learn society's expectations as a whole. Often, children imitate their favourite players when involved in sport. In so doing, they construct what Mead (1934) called the generalised other or the collectively-constructed identity of someone well-known in society. Thus, for Mead (1934), identity is clearly a construct of social interaction, not a biological concept. Identity emerges through socialisation processes. It may be the case that athlete behaviour is copied by children. Thus, athlete deviance might have a trickle-down effect.

Another interesting interactionist concept for sport socialisation is Mead's (1934) *social object*. This is a collective object which embodies a shared meaning directing a particular way of acting. The act of playing a sport with a ball is a social act with a social object; the winning of a tournament and lifting a cup in the air, similarly. This can be used to look at fandom and ritual in sport. Teams are sometimes referred to as totems to demonstrate that they are symbolic collective entities producing a unified identity. Sports consumption is a global phenomenon of group affiliation. For example, Liverpool Football Club has more than 200 Official Supporters Clubs in over 50 countries. Many studies have looked into why fans identify with a particular totem and what significance they give it (Fisher and Wakefield, 1998; Laverie and Arnett 2000; McPherson 1976). Findings indicate that it is partly the collective influence of significant others; another conclusion is that team and player identification facilitate self-esteem development (Fisher and Wakefield 1998; Laverie and Arnett 2000). This identification process is a product of socialisation processes.

Another interactionist theorist whose work has greatly influenced sport socialisation studies is Cooley (1998). His theory the Looking-Glass Self, coined in his work, *Human Nature and the Social Order* in 1902, has been particularly useful in studies on athlete identity construction. Research using this theory might look at jockeys, gymnasts and ballet dancers who suffer from eating disorders; it might also explore bodybuilders who develop muscle dysmorphia or bigorexia, a delusional obsession that one is insufficiently muscular. Specifically, Cooley's theory can be used to develop social psychology studies on the way we construct our identity through socialisation processes. He argues that we actively seek to interpret what others think about us and project that imagined judgement to create a virtual self which guides our actions. In eating disorder studies, individual's selective application of the looking glass self is analysed (Milligan and Pritchard, 2006; Rankin, 2010; Segura-García et al. 2012). Typically, it represents what individuals consider to be the ideal self. This can also be linked to the reasons why people consume goods to achieve the ideal self-concept (Landon, 1974). Fans select a product, their favourite athlete or club, and this enables them to build an identity. The link between self-image and brand-image is known as *positive self-image congruity* (Sirgy, 1982; 1985). Fans are socialised into this kind of conspicuous consumption to denote their social status (Souiden, M'Saad & Pons, 2011).

Most recently, work on social media and in particular socialising forces governing the use of Strava has been interesting. Athletes track their performances using wearable computing technology lined to satellites and then exhibit these figures on social media. However, as Smith (2017) has recently demonstrated, some are tempted to cheat by manipulating their figures to over represent themselves to boost their self-esteem, even impact their rivals. In this way, these individuals are striving to represent their ideal self. Recent research on this subject also applies Foucault's Panopticon to explore how Strava athletes are socialised away from cheating. Social media means that members are in a 'state of conscious and permanent visibility that assures the automatic functioning of power' (Foucault, 1975). The outcome of this digital gaze is that they self-discipline.

ORGANISATION OF THE BOOK

There are three sections to the book: Socialisation into sport; Socialisation out of sport: Socialisation through sport.

1. Socialisation into sport: what factors may influence initiation and continuation? In this section, the focus is on the ways a person is encouraged into sport participation as an athlete or consumer. Several examples of how ideology can socialise people into sport are presented. The second chapter explores how child athletes in China begin and live through their athletic careers. The third chapter looks at Black African Americans and how they are socialised into sport, particularly basketball and American football. The fourth chapter explores the cultures of adventure racing and dragon boating and their links to corporate culture. Today, many corporate employees are socialised into this sport as part of a process of corporate team building. The chapter ends by looking at how golf and tennis might be investigated in the same way.

2. Socialisation out of sport: what are the factors that prevent potential athletes from competing? The fifth chapter, the first in this second

section, looks at female Muslim athletes and their underrepresentation in sport (Walseth, 2006). Walseth (2006) argues that women in Muslim countries often face harassment by members of their ethnic group for sport participation as they are viewed as necessary 'symbols of cultural maintenance' (p. 91). The sixth chapter of this section looks at the way that women are being excluded from e-sports today (Loebenberg, 2018). According to Souvlis (as reported in Lane & Jackson, 2017), women make up less than 1% of the world's total eSports paid gamers and remuneration considerably differs. The seventh chapter explores the issue of intersex athletes in elite sport. This is problematic as sport is a sex-segregated milieu and one that is and remains to be, constructed on patriarchal principles and myths about sport and fairness as well as national identity and femininity. The concept of the intersex athlete fits with difficulty within the male-female binary framework.

3. Socialisation through sport: how are dimensions of identity (embodiment, gender, race, social class) developed? Sports are sites where people create and learn narratives that they use as they give meaning to and make sense of the world. The eighth chapter explores the Para-Olympics. This movement is viewed as a force for socialisation through sport as an 'advocacy body engaged through public diplomacy in promoting disability rights' (Beacom and Brittain, 2016, p. 273). This therefore looks at how sport participation can be empowering for athletes who are physically challenged. However, the chapter also looks into areas in which it can be disempowering. The next chapter explores how sport helps to redefine gender, particularly how sports like MMA are helping to show how women's sport can also be highly competitive and exciting and transcend patriarchal ideology. The tenth chapter analyses how sport participation may help to develop character e.g., sportsmanship or a set of values and attitudes that govern behaviour. Shields and Bredemeier (2001) have written that children involved in sport tend to have a better understanding of the differences between aggressive play in sport and in the playground. In contrast, some argue that sport at school, if too competitive, can lead to the development of foreclosed individuals who consistently show negative personality characteristics (see Cramer, 1995).

The conclusion rounds up the topics discussed throughout and looks to the future at other potential case studies for exploration in the field of sport socialisation.

REFERENCES

Anderson E. (2013). *"I9 and the Transformation of Youth Sport". Journal of Sport and Social Issues*, 37: 97-111

Auguet, R. (2012). *Cruelty and civilization: The Roman games*. Routledge.

Aung-Thwin, M. (2012). "Towards a national culture: Chinlone and the construction of sport in post-colonial Myanmar". *Sport in Society, 15*(10), 1341-1352.

Baker, W. J. (1988). *Sports in the western world* (Vol. 114). University of Illinois Press.

Barker, C. (2005). *Cultural Studies: Theory and Practice*. London: Sage.

Beacom, A., & Brittain, I. (2016). "Public diplomacy and the International Paralympic Committee: Reconciling the roles of disability advocate and sports regulator". *Diplomacy & Statecraft, 27*(2), 273-294.

Beal, B. (2013). *Skateboarding: the ultimate guide*. ABC-CLIO.

Beedie, P., & Craig, P. (Eds.). (2010). *Sport sociology*. London: Learning Matters.

Birrell, S. (1998). "Discourses on the gender/ sport relationship: From women in sport to gender relations". *Exercise and Sport Science Reviews, 16*, 459 – 502.

Blake, W. (1994). *Songs of Innocence and of Experience* (Vol. 2). Princeton University Press.

Bouchard, T., Lykken, D., McGue, M., Segal, N., & Tellegen, A (12 October 1990). "Sources of human psychological differences: the Minnesota Study of Twins Reared Apart". *Science.* 250 (4978): 223–228.

Brittain, I., & Beacom, A. (2016). "Leveraging the London 2012 Paralympic Games: what legacy for disabled people?" *Journal of sport and social issues, 40*(6), 499-521.

Brooke, M. (2018). The Singaporean Paralympics and Its Media Portrayal: Real Sport? Men-Only? *Communication & Sport*, 6(5), 1-20. DOI: 2167479518784278.

Burstyn, V. (1999). *The rites of men: Manhood, politics, and the culture of sport*. University of Toronto Press. Canada.

Butler, N. (2017). Exclusive: Rival groups battling to be selected as United States skateboarding national governing body by USOC. Retrieved from https://www.insidethegames.biz/articles/ 1056390/exclusive-rival-groups-battling-to-be-selected-as-united-states-skateboarding-national-governing-body-by-usoc

Chess, S, Evans, N., & Baines, J.J. (2017). "What Does a Gamer Look Like? Video Games, Advertising, and Diversity". *Journal of Television and New Media 18*(1), 37-57.

Coakley, J. J. (2009). *Sports in Society: Issues and Controversies*. Edition, 10, McGraw-Hill Education.

Constantinou, P. (2014). "Promoting Healthy competition using modified rules and sports from other cultures". *Strategies, 27*(4), 29-33.

Cooley, C. H., (1998). *Human Nature and the Social Order*. New York: Scribner's, 1902.

Dunbar RI. The social brain hypothesis. *Evol Anthropol,* (6), 78–90.

Cramer, P. (1995). "Identity, narcissism, and defence mechanisms in late adolescence". *Journal of Research in Personality, 29*(3), 341-361.

Crone, J. (1999). "Toward a theory of sport". *Journal of sport behavior, 22*(3), 321-340.

Dubbert, J.L. (1979). *A man's place: Masculinity in transition*. Englewood Cliffs, NJ: Prentice-Hall.

Dunbar, R. (1996). *Gossip, grooming and the evolution of language*. Cambridge: Harvard UP.

Dunbar, R. I. (1998). "The social brain hypothesis". *Brain, 9*(10), 178-190.

Eagleton, T. (2007). *The meaning of life*. Oxford University Press. Oxford.

Elias, N. (2000). *The Civilizing Process: Sociogenetic and Psychogenetic Investigations*. Trans. Edmund Jephcott (rev. ed). Oxford: Blackwell.

Elster, J. (1989). *Nuts and bolts for the social sciences*. Cambridge University Press.

Fisher, R. J., & Wakefield, K. (1998). "Factors leading to group identification: A field study of winners and losers". *Psychology & Marketing, 15*(1), 23-40.

Foucault, M. (1975). *Discipline and punish: The birth of the prison*. NY: Vintage.

Frost, J. L. (1992). *Play and playscapes*. New York: Delmar Albany.

Gramsci, A. (1971). *Selections from the Prison Notebooks of Antonio Gramsci.* Ed. and Transl. by Quintin Hoare and Geoffrey Nowell Smith. New York: International Publishers.

Griggs, G. (2009). "The origins and development of ultimate frisbee". *The sport journal, 12*(3).

Hamari J., & Sjöblom M. (2017). "What is eSports and why do people watch it?" *Internet Research, 27*(2), 211-232

Hoberman, J. M. (2001). *Mortal engines: The science of performance and the dehumanization of sport.* Blackburn Press.

Hong, F. (2004). "Innocence Lost: Child Athletes in China". *Sport in Society, 7*(3), 338-354

Huizinga, J. (1955). *Homo ludens; a study of the play-element in culture.* Boston: Beacon Press.

Landon L., (1974). "Self-Concept, Ideal Self-Concept and Consumer Purchase Intentions". *Journal of Consumer Research. 1*(2), 44-51.

Lane, S and Jackson, E. (2017). "Female gamers face sexism and bullying in e-sports competitions", *ABC.* Retrieved from http://www.abc.net.au/radio/programs/am/female-gamers-face-sexism-and-bullying-in-e-sports/8516486

Laverie, D. A., & Arnett, D. B. (2000). "Factors affecting fan attendance: The influence of identity salience and satisfaction". *Journal of leisure Research, 32*(2), 225-246.

Leberman, S., Collins, C., & Trenberth, L. (2012). "The sport business industry". In *Sport business management in New Zealand and Australia* (3rd ed., pp. 2–22).

Ledwith, M. (2009). "Antonio Gramsci and feminism: The elusive nature of power". *Educational Philosophy and Theory, 41*(6), 684-697.

Loy, L. & Coakley, J. (2009). "Sport". *Blackwell Encyclopedia of Sociology.* Blackwell Publishing.

Marx, K. *Economic and Philosophic Manuscripts of 1844.* Progress Publishers, Moscow 1959.

———. (1867). *Das Kapital.* The General Law of Capitalist Accumulation. Vol. 1, Ch. 25. Retrieved from https://www.marxists.org/archive/marx/works/1867-c1/ch25.htm

McPherson, B. D. (1976). "Socialization into the role of sport consumer: A theory and causal model". *Canadian Review of Sociology/Revue canadienne de sociologie, 13*(2), 165-177.

Mead, G. H. (1934). *Mind, self & society from the standpoint of a social behaviourist* (Edited by C. W. Morris). Chicago, IL: University of Chicago Press.

Messner, M. A. (1988). "Sports and male domination: The female athlete as contested ideological terrain". *Sociology of sport journal, 5(3),* 197-211.

Messner, M. (2002). *Taking the field: Women, men and sports.* Minneapolis: University of Minnesota Press.

Milligan, B. & Pritchard, M. (2006). "The Relationship between Gender, Type of Sport, Body Dissatisfaction, Self Esteem and Disordered Eating Behaviors in Division I Athletes. Athletic insight". *The Online Journal of Sport Psychology, 8,* 32-46.

Misztal, B. A. (2003). "Durkheim on collective memory". *Journal of Classical Sociology, 3*(2), 123-143.

Morales, M. (2014). "Tennis' Gender Pay Gap Problem Looms on The Side-lines". *Forbes.* Retrieved from https://www.forbes.com/sites/miguelmorales/2014/02/21/tennis-gender-pay-gap-problem-looms-on-the-sidelines/#466ee9c471dd

Pinker, S. (1994). *The language instinct. How the mind creates language.* William Morrow and Company. US.

Prescott, J. & Bogg, J. (2013). "The gendered identity of women working in the computer games industry". *Eludamos, Journal for Computer Game Culture, 7*(1), 55-67.

Rankin, J. W. (2010). "Making Weight in Sports". In L. Burke & V. Deakin (Eds.). *Clinical Sports Nutrition* (4th ed., pp. 149-170). New South Wales: McGraw-Hill.

Rice, J. (2010). "Perils of financial planning". *ESPN.* Retrieved from http://www.espn.com/action/skateboarding/story/_/id/7547702/pro-skaters-try-overcome-obstacles-financial-planning.

Rousseau, J. J. (1992). *Discourse on the Origin of Inequality*. Translated by Donald Cress. Indianapolis: Hackett Publishing Company.

Scraton, S., & Flintoff, A. (2013). "Gender, Feminist Theory, and Sport". In D. L. Andrews, & B. Carrington (Eds) *Companion to Sport* (pp. 96-111). Oxford, United Kingdom: Blackwell Publishing Ltd.

Scott, J., & Marshall, G. (Eds.). (2009). *A dictionary of sociology*. Oxford University Press, USA.

Segura-Garcìa C, Papaianni MC, Caglioti F, Procopio L, Nisticò CG, Bombardiere L, Ammendolia A, Rizza P, De Fazio P, Capranica L. (2012). "Orthorexia nervosa: a frequent eating disordered behavior in athletes". *Eat Weight Disord*, 17: e226-e233.

Sewart, J. J. (1987). "The commodification of sport". *International Review for the Sociology of Sport*, *22*(3), 171-192.

Shields, D. L., & Bredemeier, B. (2001). "Moral development and behavior in sport". *Handbook of sport psychology*, *2*, 585-603.

Shields, D. L., & Bredemeier, B. L. (2010). "Competition: Was Kohn, right?" *Phi Delta Kappan, 91*(5), 62-67.

Sirgy, M. J. (1982). "Self-Concept in Consumer Behavior: A Critical Review". *Journal of Consumer Research, 9*(3), 287-300.

———. (1985). "Using self-congruity and ideal congruity to predict purchase motivation". *Journal of Business Research*, 13, 195-206.

Smith, W. R. (2017). "Communication, sportsmanship, and negotiating ethical conduct on the digital playing field". *Communication & Sport, 5*(2), 160-185.

Souiden, N., M'Saad, B., & Pons, F. (2011). "A cross-cultural analysis of consumers' conspicuous consumption of branded fashion accessories". *Journal of International Consumer Marketing, 23*(5), 329-343.

Strinati, D. (1995). "Marxism, political economy and ideology". *An Introduction to Theories of Popular Culture*, pp. 127-76.

Thornton, A. (2004). "Anyone can play this game: Ultimate Frisbee, identity and difference". In B. Wheaton, (Ed.). (2004). *Understanding lifestyle sport: Consumption, identity and difference*. Routledge, (pp. 175-196).

West, E.G. (2003). "Property rights in the history of economic thought: From Locke to J. S. Mill". In T. L. Anderson & F. S. McChesney (Eds.), *Property rights: Cooperation, conflict, and law* (pp. 20-42). Princeton, NJ: Princeton University Press.

Whiten A, Byrne R, (1997). *Machiavellian Intelligence II: Extensions and Evaluations*. Cambridge, UK: Cambridge University Press.

Yeam, C. T. & Brooke, M. (2016): "Changing perceptions of disability through sport: the case of Singaporean wheelchair basketball", *Asia Pacific Journal of Sport and Social Science*, 5, (3), 1-8.

PART 1:

SOCIALISATION INTO SPORT

CHAPTER 2

Child Athletes in the People's Republic of China

In the introduction, reference was made to Mead (1934)'s *social object* and it was argued that a collective object can embody a shared meaning directing a particular way of acting. One such object is the gold medal of the Olympic champion, particularly for the powerful developed nations such as the US, Russia and China; another is the football FIFA World Cup. Each of these are the catalysts for this analysis of China's recent sporting aspirations. They provide the context for the investigation of China's sports schools and why children are socialised into sport at an early age.

China's state ideology on the importance of achieving success in the Olympics has been summed up by Wu Shaozu, the Minister of Sport from 1990 to 2000:

> 'The highest aim of Chinese sport is success in the Olympic Games. We must concentrate our resources on it. To raise the flag at the Olympics is our major responsibility' (cited in Hong et al. 2005, p. 514).

In the same way, the current President Xi Jin-Ping declared, in 2009, that he intended to promote elite football in China with the objective of ultimately winning the FIFA World Cup. Hong et al. (2005) have argued that the worth of the Olympic gold medal is based on 'political objectives' (p. 518); further, they state that this has been the case for many decades. Tan et al. (2016) point out similar reasoning behind winning the FIFA World Cup. Sport is evidently a way for China to be seen as one of the dominant world powers.

The desire to succeed on the World's sporting stage can be seen to have developed extensively in the Maoist era, between 1949 and 1978. Sport had a central political role: to demonstrate that capitalism was inferior. Another reason for the development is because the Chinese have, for many decades, bemoaned the oppression of their civilisation by the West and Japan. As Hong et al. (2005) point out, there is a well-known ancient dictum in China: 'A winner is a king, a loser is nothing but a bandit' (*chengzhe wanghou baizhekou*). Saving face translates as *ai mian zi* in pinyin. The Chinese are deeply afraid of losing face in public (Jinxia and Mangan, 2001). The Chinese also nostalgically reminisce about the strength of the Imperial Tang Dynasty (618–907), the second largest and longest-enduring empire. Success in sport reflects the 'sleeping giants''s reemergence. It represents a strong socializing power. After China's successes at the Athens Olympics, a journalist in the People's Daily (2004) wrote:

> 'When a country is powerful, its sport will flourish. Chinese athletes' excellent performance at the Olympic stage is inevitably proof of our great

achievements in economic reform and modernization. Chinese athletes will make more contributions to realize our nation's great revival' (as cited in Lu and Hong, 2013, p. 110).

Having experienced 20 years of Deng Xiaoping's open-door policy, it seemed that China's revival was truly taking shape with investment from the International Olympic Committee from television rights and corporate sponsorship (Forbes (2008, https://www.forbes.com/2008/04/23/chinaolympicssponsorsopedcx_sre_0424olympic s.html) from 11 global sponsors, including Coca-Cola and McDonald's. For the reasons above, the Chinese have made sport an integral part of their political society and it is clear that young athletes in China are socialised into sport for ideological reasons. The identity given to a gold medal winner is one of a state hero and is therefore a very powerful motivator for a would-be professional elite athlete.

Althusser (1971) argues that ideology can be seen in individuals' actions not just their beliefs. However, those actions are 'defined by the material ideological apparatus from which we derive the ideas of that subject' (p. 158-159). Althusser (1971) posits that individuals are subject to *interpellation* or *hailed* by the system; in these cases, the Olympic gold medal and the FIFA World Cup discourses are propagated by the state. These discourses that lead citizens into roles that the state requires are termed by Althusser as forces of the *Ideological State Apparatus*. In order to accrue the resources required to develop Olympic and World Cup aspirations, senior officials in the State Council of China collaborated directly with private corporations for patronage. Tan et al. (2016) thus conclude that what we see in China's case is a model of State Corporatism whereby the government seeks to 'achieve national objectives through mandatory social cooperation' (p. 1451). In other words, citizens are socialised into agreement with the Party's wishes.

The system developed by the Chinese to achieve national objectives, namely, to succeed at the Olympics, is called the *Juguo Tizhi* scheme, which means the 'nationwide support for an elite-sport system'. In 1979, China's sports policy could be seen to focus on developing elite sport first, then general sport for all. It was only from 1995, that sport for all, with the National Fitness Programme, was prioritised. This provided the platform for investment in elite sport and particularly to winning medals. Today, the Chinese government spends colossal amounts on athletes and coaches for success in international tournaments. Similarly, China has high hopes for its football aspirations and has invested considerably in the infrastructure to do so. Li Liyan, a General Administration of Sports researcher has estimated that China has spent, on average, 700 million yuan ($103 million) to win each Olympic gold medal (last accessed China Daily, June 2017, http://www.chinadaily.com.cn/opinion/2010-04/08/content_9700301.htm). From winning 15 gold medals at the 1992 Barcelona Olympics, China climbed to first place with 48 golds at the 2008 Beijing Games and 2nd in London with 38 and 3rd in Rio with 26 golds.

The Olympic medal-oriented policy is based on a 'human ladder' concept. The premise is that over time, a pyramid of selection will socialise out the weaker elements. From around 400, 000 young athletes in sports schools in China, about 4,000 will make the cut to become Olympic athletes. About 95% of the gold medallists derive from these 4000 (Goh, 2016). They are known as *Zhuanye* athletes and are government subsidised. They are examples of sporting civil servants and can be viewed differently to those athletes who are deemed professional but paid by their employers, for example, their football team. The *Zhuanye* athletes are the Olympic medal aspirations and are at the summit. These athletes are socialised into the sporting field and trained from a young age, often starting as early as 6 years (Jones, 2012). Thus, success is said to not only be due to the centralised management and the guaranteed allocation of resources but also the age of the recruits.

The Chinese Football League was established in 1992 and the Chinese Football Association (CFA) set up with a First Division divided into two groups: A (15 teams) and B (12 teams). Although the CFA is classed as a non-governmental body, it is still closely tied to the state. As in other football systems, the first two professional teams of B group are promoted to replace the two bottom teams of A each season. These teams can mainly be found in urban areas on the Eastern side of China. Clubs are franchise controlled but the CFA is a member of the State Sport General Administration of China. It therefore acts in accordance with state policy. Similarly, to the sports schools in China for Olympic success, there are a great deal of youth schools for football. Additionally, in 2015, the Chinese government made football a component of the national school curriculum. The goal is to develop training programmes in 20,000 Chinese schools and to produce 100,000 new players able to play professionally.

Conceived and funded by property tycoon Xu Jiayin, the Evergrande Football School boasts 2,800 pupils aged nine to 16 and 167 acres containing 50 pitches (http://www.scmp.com/news/china/society/article/1946164/chinese-football-will-never-be-same-again-how-worlds-biggest). It is the result of a $185 million investment and is the largest soccer school in the world. Its objective is to develop China's soccer talent and its status and transform china from its current 86th position into a leading soccer power. Its motto is 'Boosting China's football and cultivating football stars' (http://time.com/2901783/worlds-biggest-soccer-football-academy-china/).

Coaches recommend, or scouts travelling the length and breadth of the country discover, sporting talents. In an interview, Olympic historian David Wallechinsky argued that the Chinese scout the country 'looking for children of certain body types and going to their parents and getting them to send them to national training centres' (http://factsanddetails.com/china/cat12/sub79/item1008.html). Each governmental district comprises sport scouts and doctors who look for and assess children from ages 8 to 13 as potential candidates for sports schools. Physiological assessments by doctors on factors such as height, arm span, bone density and flexibility are carried out to determine which sports these youngsters may excel in. If, after these assessments, these children demonstrate good potential for further development, they may be transferred immediately to a sports school. Related to this system, Ching Ching writes:

> 'When I was in the first grade, scouts from the Communist sports machinery came to our school to hunt for future champions. The event was diving.

Never mind that I couldn't swim and had no desire to be an athlete, I was told I had the right proportions and good feet. Chosen from a field of thousands to train at a state sports school, I was supposed to be thrilled to serve my country' (http://factsanddetails.com/china/cat12/sub79/item1008.html).

Having spent several years in their local sporting environment, they might be selected and transit to a large government training academy in their teens. Hayes (2008) cites the experiences of 2 professional Chinese athletes Liu Huana and Yao Min, gathered from interviews. Liu Huana, one of China's national women's soccer players, stated:

'I had never heard of soccer until I was 13, when I moved to the county for my fifth-grade studies. One day people from the local athletic school came to our school to select new members. The teacher recommended me because I was the fastest runner in the class. I wore a skirt and sandal shoes that day, and I just took off my shoes and ran' (http://factsanddetails.com/china/cat12/sub79/item1008.html).

Famous basketball player Yao Ming joined a sports academy at 12. Based on measurements of his knuckles, it was predicted that he would grow to be 7 foot five and therefore an ideal height for basketball and a future star player. However, Yao stated that he did not like playing basketball until he reached the age of 18. He also remarked that his 'parents would probably prefer for me to go to college and play basketball only as a hobby' (http://factsanddetails.com/china/cat12/sub79/item1008. html). Yao was clearly socialised unwillingly into the sport.

Some children may be enrolled by their parents for approximately $100 a year. Some parents may be ambitious for their children; others may think this is an indirect way for their child to gain a functional education and to be nurtured in a healthier environment than they themselves can provide. Additionally, the whole family can benefit; the local sports bureaux often provide homes for the parents of potential elite athletes.

Wu Yigang, a Shanghai University professor declares that the Chinese sports school system is

'very good at finding sports talent. It meets the demand of our nation to make achievements in a very short time. However, the "Chinese way of training is problematic. These schools emphasize only training and neglect everything else. It greatly affects children's knowledge and their moral outlook' http://factsanddetails.com/china/cat12/sub79/item1008.html.

Indeed, there is criticism that children do not spend enough time on academics. One 15-year-old runner at Weifang City Sports School told Time "I run, and I sleep" That's my day (http://factsanddetails.com/china/cat12/sub79/item1008.html). Other young children perform rigorous drills on mats throughout the day.

The *Juguo Tizhi* advocates elite performance by specialising its athletes early. Cote et. Al., (2007) explain deliberate practice to be:

'Any training activity (a) undertaken with the specific purpose of increasing performance, (b) requiring cognitive and/or physical effort, and (c) relevant to promoting positive skill development' (p.2).

The question that emerges is whether this genre of early specialisation is an effective one over the long term. The *Developmental Model of Sport Participation* by Cote et al. (2007) provides insights into the *Juguo Tizhi* and as to whether it is a good system. The first years of training tend to comprise repetitive drills and very little time spent practising the sport the child has been selected for. For example, potential archers begin the first year without arrows, solely pulling the string back, holding it for a lengthy period, and then releasing it, to develop the required muscle mass. This practice might be criticised for being needlessly monotonous and gruelling (Jacobs, 2012). Early specialisation programmes consisting of very long days of repetitive training schedules may lead to athletes leaving their sport due to injury or burn out. Youth soccer academies focus on deliberate practice to increase performance standards. Under the elite *Juguo Tizhi* sport system, child athletes are consistently pressurised to withstand hardship and pain, as part of their training (Hong, 2004). There is a high level of discipline which proponents argue is a necessary evil to achieve the performance requirements that China has witnessed. Journalist Mimi Lau from the SCMP reports:

'Life is not easy on campus, with the pupils on a tight schedule from dawn to dusk that's packed with football training, matches and school lessons' http://www.scmp.com/news/china/society/article/1946164/chinese-football-will-never-be-same-again-how-worlds-biggest.

This focus on hardship, even abuse, is a reflection of the traditional Chinese belief that only through enduring can an individual achieve (Hong, 2004). However, there is substantial evidence to prove that early specialisation is followed by a reduction in enjoyment and physical health (Cote et. al, 2007). This excess increases the risk of overuse injuries (Caine et al. 1989) and means that these youngsters are more susceptible to burnout and depression (Malina, 2009).

Further, this system of taking young children from their families to train them to be professional elite athletes is a highly controversial one and recently has received a great deal of criticism. It is evident that there are human rights issues with *Juguo Tizhi* in terms of the psychological and physical well-being of the athletes. UNESCO reports that 'top-class sport and sport practice by all must be protected against any abuse. It is important that all sport authorities and sportsmen and women be conscious of the risks, and more especially to children, of precocious and inappropriate training and psychological pressure of every kind' (UNESCO, 1978, retrieved http://www.unesco.org/education/pdf/SPORT_E.PDF).

The children undergo very harsh conditions in the *Juguo Tizhi* scheme, with up to 10 hours of training per day (Hong, 2004). There have been cases reported of coach abuse (Calvin, 2012), and the doping of these children (Hong, 2004). Coaches like Ma Junren, renowned for abusive behavior have been honoured (Hong, 2004). Other abuses relate to the way these children are detached from their families. For example, the father of Olympic gold medallist Lin Qing Feng admitted that he had not seen his son over seven years building up to the London Olympics (New York Times, 2012 http://www. nytimes.com/2012/08/08/sports/olympics/chinas-quest-for-olympic-gold-takes-toll-on-athletes.html). His only glimpse of him was on the television. He told a Shanghai newspaper: "We accepted a long time ago that he doesn't belong to us. I don't even dare think about things like enjoying family happiness". Further, diver and three-time Olympic gold medal, Wu Minxia reported that her mother's death was not divulged to her until after her competition to safeguard her Olympic prospects. Similarly, Wu was sent to a state-financed sports academy when she was young. The documentary Little Big Dreams created by *Nurture* https://www.youtube.com/watch?v=ZtS9RSPDpJs in 2015 depicts the everyday existence of 100 of these children who travel from all over China to the infamous Li Xiaoshuang Gymnastic School in an attempt to become Olympic stars. The documentary explores the harshness of the regime and the difficulties the children face with the teachers and without their parents. With the very young age of the children and the very long hours that they commit, parallels between child athletes and child labour have been drawn. The children are said to suffer in a milieu where working conditions are inhumane (Hong, 2004, p.341).

Additionally, because only a select few become members of the national and Olympic teams, very many of these nurtured athletes leave the sports schools lacking other avenues for success (Hong et al. 2005, p.521). Some former athletes become coaches or find employment in sport associations; others sell sporting equipment or promote athletic centers. However, many end up unemployed. They might be restricted by physical injury and they may lack a functional education because the Chinese sporting industry lacks career contingency plans (Hong, 2004, p.344). It appears that 240,000 athletes have retired and are living with injuries, poverty and unemployment. Xu refers to these ex-elites as China's 'disposable athletes'. Indeed, a former gold medal gymnast, Zhang Shangwu, was found begging on the streets of Beijing (http://www.telegraph.co.uk/news/worldnews/asia/china/8645237/Top-Chinese-gymnast-found-begging-on-the-street.html). A local track-and-field coach told Newsweek, "When these kids leave athletic schools, they can't do anything; they have no skills. Local sports commissions sometimes provide jobs, but in the end, many become factory workers."

Cote et al. (2007) have demonstrated, through a great many cases, that sport sampling at an early age is much more effective. These authors argue that exploring a diverse range of sports is more impactful for youngsters. Children should be encouraged to engage in various sport forms and they should be enabled to enjoy these activities. Thus, from the outset, choices to participate in sport are more autonomous and focused on the element of play. This relates back to the introduction and the importance of play as presented by Huizinga and the ubiquity of sport in our societies as a social activity. 'Deliberate play is intrinsically motivating as it is done for enjoyment' (Côté et al. 2007, pp. 185-6). Additionally, through their research, Cote et al. (2007) found that children are more voluntarily willing to become involved in intense, more repetitive training practice at an older age if they have had the opportunity to sample several activities for enjoyment. Indeed, many elite athletes only began specialising in their career at a later age. Hakeem Olajuwon, for example, a National Basketball Association athlete from 1984 to 2002, and part of basketballs' Hall of Fame had not begun playing basketball until the age of 15. Before that, he was more engaged in American football. Elite performance through sampling can provide the same outcome but without the risks of burnout or injury due to repetitive deliberate practice activities. Hence, socialisation into sport as predominantly deliberate practice at an early age, may not be effective.

Strudwick (2016) presents how deliberate play may help nurture football elites. Three main areas of excellence are essential: physiological characteristics, particularly anaerobic and endurance capacity; technical skills; and tactical skills. This final element is rarely learned without the opportunity to play a football game, during which the cognitive capabilities to make quick and accurate decisions in an unpredictable situation, can be trained. Therefore, a focus on deliberate practice may only be effective in developing the other two skills required for elite sporting success. Through deliberate play activities, children can 'experiment with different movements' (Côté et al., 2007, p. 186). The current training of the *Juguo Tizhi* scheme may be at odds with this. It might be that some are beginning to understand that these research findings are important.

Recently, there has been a shift in the support for this sport policy and a reduction in enrolment in recent years (Song et. al, 2016). Parents have developed more awareness about their children's educational needs and today are not as prone to voluntarily offer them to the state for training. Document 23 has been the result of this trend stipulating that sports schools must modify their operations by placing more focus on the academic side and the welfare of their athletes (Song et. al, 2016). Thus, the Chinese government has been socialised into implementing a similar programme to the one the N.C.A.A. operates. This is exemplified by cases such as Yu Fen, whose scheme at Tsinghua University in Beijing, is careful to provide a sound education.

Finally, from a wider perspective, the process of developing a national football youth culture cannot rely on academies of this ilk. According to a journalist at The Huffington Post (2016), interest for basketball is still significantly greater than for football in China. One predominant reason for this, is the lack of a culture of playing football out of interest and fun. A greater number of children might be involved in football, if it could become more popular at the grassroots level. This is in line with Côté et al.'s (2007) point that involvement in deliberate play 'would have a positive effect over time on an individual's overall motivation and ultimately the individual's willingness to engage in more externally controlled activities' (p.187). In other words, in time, having sampled a diverse number of sports and chosen one as a preference, children grow up and develop to intrinsically desire deliberate practice so that they can improve their skills. It is important that forces are in place to socialise children into football with a play function to begin with.

To conclude, China has a history of socializing children into sport at a very early age. Using Mead (1934)'s social object, it is possible to view how sport represents this society's main goal of demonstrating to the world that it is a superpower. This is why Althusser (1971)'s notion of interpellation or being hailed by the system, can also be applied. Would-be Olympic champions are highly sought-after by the state to answer the call to succeed. However, abusive practices have been uncovered in the system. Stories abound of young children's experiences of living away from their familiies for long periods. Also, training practices in sports schools have been heavily criticised as they appear to be at odds with human rights. Additionally, many athletes end up unemployed as the schools do not prepare their chidren with an education for their post-athletic days. Moreover, the logic of these practices is questioned as early specialisation has been shown to lack substantial sound evidence that it leads to success (Cote et al., 2007). Therefore, these practices can be criticised at the scientific as well as the ethical level. On a more positive note, more recent institutions appear to acknowledge the importance of providing students with an education and this is coupled with a reduction in the number of very early starters being socialised into sport by the regime. These are welcome changes and perhaps trends that will continue to grow as China becomes more visible to the world through its structural developments.

REFERENCES

Althusser, L. (1971). "Ideology and Ideological State Apparatuses". *Lenin and Philosophy and other Essays*. pp.121–176.

Baker, J., Schorer, J., & Cobley, S. (Eds.). (2012). *Talent identification and development in sport: International perspectives*. Routledge.

Caine, D., Cochrane, B., Caine, C., & Zemper, E. (1989). « An epidemiologic investigation of injuries affecting young competitive female gymnasts". *American Journal of Sports Medicine, 17*, 811–820.

Calvin, M. (2012). "The Last Word: Lives given up in the pursuit of gold medals". *The Independent*. Retrieved from http://www.independent.co.uk/sport/olympics/comment/the-last-word-lives-given-up-in-the-pursuit-of-gold-medals-8007902.html.

Cote J., Baker J. & Abernethy B. (2007). "Practice and Play in the Development of Sport Expertise". In Tenebaum G. and Eklund R. C. (Eds.), *Handbook of Sport Psychology*. Pp. 184-198. Hoboken, New Jersey: John Wiley & Sons Inc.

CNN. (2016). "Guangzhou Evergrande: Inside China's $185M football factory". Retrieved from http://edition.cnn.com/2016/03/15/football/football-china-guangzhou-evergrande/

Goh, B. (2016). "China rethinks its sporting obsession as Rio Olympics approach". Retrieved from http://www.reuters.com/article/us-olympics-rio-china-school-idUSKCN0Y932W

Guthrie, D. (1999). *Dragon in a three-piece suit: the emergence of capitalism in China*, Princeton, NJ: Princeton University Press.

Hong, F. (2004). "Innocence Lost: Child Athletes in China". *Sport in Society, 7*(3), 338-354

Hong, F., Wu P. & Xiong H. (2005). "Beijing Ambitions: An Analysis of the Chinese Elite Sports System and its Olympic Strategy for the 2008 Olympic Games". *The International Journal of the History of Sport, 22*(4), 510-529.

Jacobs, A. (2012). "China's Quest for Olympic Gold Takes Toll on Athletes". *The New York Times*. Retrieved from https://www.nytimes.com/2012/08/ 08/sports/olympics/chinas-quest-for-olympic-gold-takes-toll-on-athletes.html

Jinxia D. & Mangan, J.A. (2001). "Football in the New China: Political Statement, Entrepreneurial Enticement and Patriotic Passion", *Soccer & Society*, 2:3, 79-100

Jones D. (2012). "Ye Shiwen: forging of the Mandarin mermaid". How Chinese children are brutalised into future Olympia. *Daily Mail*. Retrieved from http://www.dailymail.co.uk/news/article-2181374/Ye-Shiwen--forging-Mandarin-mermaid-How-Chinese-children-brutalised-future-Olympians.html.

Lu, Z., & Hong, F. (2013). *Sport and nationalism in China*. Routledge: London.

Malina, R. M. (2009). "Children and adolescents in the sport culture: The overwhelming majority to the select few". *Journal of Exercise Science & Fitness, 7*(2), S1-S10

Mead, G. H. (1934). *Mind, self & society from the standpoint of a social behaviourist* (Edited by C. W. Morris). Chicago, IL: University of Chicago Press.

Schmitter P.C & Lehmbruch, G. (1979). *Trends Toward Corporatist Intermediation,* London: Sage.

Song A., Sajolj D. & Goh, B. (2016). "China's sport schools losing their shine". *The Straits Times*. Retrieved from https://www.straitstimes.com/asia/east-asia/fading-glory

Strudwick, A. (2016). *Soccer Science*. Human Kinetics: UK.

Tan, T. C., Huang, H-C., Bairner, A. & Chen, Y-W. (2016). "Xi Jin-Ping's World Cup Dreams: From a Major Sports Country to a World Sports Power", *The International Journal of the History of Sport*, 33:12, 1449-1465

The Huffington Post. (2016). *Chinese Soccer's Lofty Goals*. Retrieved from http://www.huffingtonpost.com/china-hands/chinese-soccers-lofty-goa_b_9856918.html

Wu Shaozu, Zhonghua renmin gongheguo tiyu shi (zonghe juan) ['Sports History in the PRC'] (Beijing: Zhongguo shuji chubanshe, 1999), pp.402–4.

'Wuxing hongqi wo wei ni jiao'ao: relie zhuhe woguo tiyu jianer zai aoyunhui shang qude youyi chengji' ['I Am Proud of the Five Starred Red Flag: Congratulations for the Victory of Our National Sports Heroes in Athens'], Renmin ribao, 30 Aug. 2004, 1.

Xu, J. (2007). China's Disposable Athletes. *Time*. Retrieved from http://content.time. com/time/world/article/0,8599,1644120,00.html.

CHAPTER 3

Race and Social Channelling of African Americans into Sport

Back in 1994, Herrnstein and Murray (1994) posited that this sporting dominance of African Americans was widely celebrated by the Black community in the US and seen as a positive group identifier source. It appears to be the same today also with the numbers in the NFL and NBA. Beamon and Messner (2014) point out that African American men comprise a staggering 67% of American football and 78% of basketball teams. To explain this, here has been a genetic argument manufactured revealing differences between Black and white athletes. In 2003, research from Yang et al. (2003) on the *ACTN3* gene, found that an individual might be naturally predisposed toward specialist performance in sprint and power events such as basketball and American football. With the statistics of African domination in power sport, it is rational to believe such a claim. However, in 2011, this finding was overturned. Eynon et al. (2011) convincingly demonstrate that it is highly unlikely this genotype has any influence on muscle fibers that generate power and speed. Hence, insofar as genetics are concerned, there is no proof that athletes of African descent are superior.

At the same time, with the positive accounts of high levels of Black elite sport participation and potential genetic superiority today, racial segregation in American cities is an alarming issue in America. A large proportion of African American children tend to live in ghettos and poverty is significant. Statistics from Austin (2013) at the US Economic Policy Institute, demonstrate that 'nearly half (45%) of poor Black children live in neighbourhoods with concentrated poverty, but only a little more than a tenth (12%) of poor white children live in similar neighbourhoods' (http://www.epi.org/publication/african-americans-concentrated-neighborhoods/)

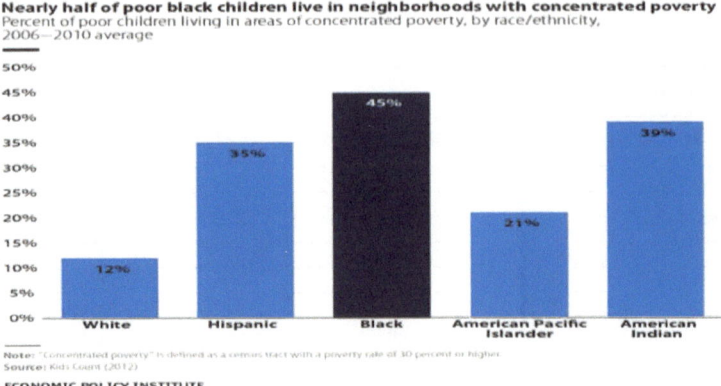

Nearly half of poor black children live in neighborhoods with concentrated poverty
Percent of poor children living in areas of concentrated poverty, by race/ethnicity, 2006—2010 average

Note: "Concentrated poverty" is defined as a census tract with a poverty rate of 30 percent or higher.
Source: Kids Count (2012)

ECONOMIC POLICY INSTITUTE

Typically, growing up in an area like this, means fewer opportunities for economic and social mobility. As Delpit (2012) demonstrates, African American males are the lowest achievers in education; the highest perpetrators and victims of homicides; represent the biggest increase in suicide; have declined in life expectancy; contract HIV/AIDS more than the other ethnic groups in America; and are the least successful on the job front.

Authors (Beamon, 2010; Beamon & Bell, 2006; 2011) have explained that high levels of African American participation in sports, such as basketball and American football, are clearly due to a sports socialisation process in the African American families and neighborhoods, and that this can be linked to the above-mentioned depiction from Delpit (2012). She uses Social Learning Theory from Bandura (1963) to explain how the acquisition of culturally appropriate behaviour occurs in an individual's environment through primary and secondary sources such as the family, peers and the media. The in-depth ethnographic interviews with former African American collegiate athletes that she conducts demonstrate that sport, above other roles or skills, is emphasised as a career path from early in life. This corroborates Edwards' (2000) argument that for Blacks, there are few role models outside the field of sport. Beamon (2010) uses the term social channeling to explain this process. It is very similar to Althusser's interpellation. Poor African American families are encouraged to improve their status through sport. In this way, they are hailed into becoming subjects that 'possess higher expectations for professional sports careers as a means to upward mobility and economic viability' (p. 281) than their white counterparts. Bonilla-Silva (2014) identifies this as one of the frames of colour-blindness with the belief that America is a meritocratic society and each citizen has equal opportunity to success. This frame fails to entertain the socio-political and sociohistorical difficulties that this minority group faces.

For White supremacy to be maintained, there is what Bourdieu (1986) refers to as Cultural Reproduction, which helps the racism of the White capitalist system to seem fair. Cultural Reproduction is maintained systemically through sport. Hoberman (1997) points out that Murray and Herrnstein's encouragement of the Black community to celebrate its strength in the sporting environment is, in fact, destructive

(p. 3). It creates 'a clan pride based on rejecting intellectual role models' Hoberman (1997, p. 3). In school achievement, it is a fact that African American males have very poor statistics. They are consistently underperforming and are more likely to be expelled or to be classified as having a learning or emotional disability. Professor Shaun Harper, founder of the Center for the Study of Race and Equity in Education at the University of Pennsylvania, and his colleagues (2013) show that merely 2.8% of full-time undergraduate students are of African American descent and those are oftentimes allocated 'paper classes'. In the case of University of North Carolina, students were awarded B's and A's to remain in their respective teams, not as true reflections of their studies (Lyall, 2014). Further, the topics of courses are often not aimed at steering these students into potentially powerful social roles in institutions such as Law, Politics or Business, which are clearly vocationally-oriented. Examples studied by the athletes are Swahili and African American History. Additionally, according to Harper et al. (2013), college admissions for these athletes was far from normal:

> 'There were too few young Black men who met admissions standards and were sufficiently prepared for the rigors of college-level academic work [and] despite these arguments, colleges and universities somehow manage to find academically qualified Black male student-athletes to play on revenue-generating sports teams' (p. 17).

They conclude that young Black men comprised 2.8% of undergraduate students in university but 57.1% of the men's football and 64.3% of the men's basketball teams. Further, due to a very poor stipend, many tend to drop out before graduation due to financial difficulties or due to the hardship of juggling their study and sport commitments. Jacobs (2015) reports that many student-athletes are practising 40 hours a week. Moreover, only around $600 million of the $50 billion provided for scholarships is given over for athletic scholarships.

Some argue that there could be a shift in consciousness if youngsters were more aware that they might succeed through academics (Jacobs, 2015). In reality, what is created is a triple tragedy:

> 'One, the tragedy of thousands upon thousands of Black youths in the obsessive pursuit of sports goals that the overwhelming majority of them will never attain. Two, the tragedy of the personal and cultural underdevelopment that afflicts so many successful and unsuccessful Black sports aspirants. Three, the tragedy of cultural and institutional underdevelopment throughout Black society as a consequence of the drain in talent potential toward sports and away from other vital areas of occupational and career emphasis such as medicine, law, economics, politics, education, and technical fields' (Harrison, 2000, p. 36 as cited in Beamon, p. 351).

In comparison to Whites, African-American males are socialised by family, communities and media into certain sports, particularly basketball and American football. This limits exposure to, and desire for, other career paths (Beamon, 2010; Edwards, 2000; Harris, 1994; Beamon and Messner, 2014).

In addition to the family and neighborhood, another socialising agent is the media. Kane (1995) states that 'the mass media have become one of the most powerful institutional forces for shaping values and attitudes in modern culture' (pp. 88–89). Additionally, sport has become the world's most diverse cultural common denominator with more space devoted to it in popular culture mediums than any other topic, including politics. *Sports Illustrated* in America has a circulation of around 23 million each week giving power to this source of popular culture. Within these sources, there is a very extensive and consistent photographic portrayal of successful athletes; often these images are used to endorse products. It propagates ideological discourses that impact the reality of the Black African American's social life. The media reinforces the popular ideology concerning sport participation and dismissing African Americans from academic success. For their research, Goss et al. (2009) analyze 216 cover pages portraying NBA players, with photographs and written texts, from Sports Illustrated from 1970 to 2003. Their content analysis explored differences in portrayal of Black and White athletes. They research whether, during this period, Black athletes were more likely to be presented as having natural abilities. They conclude that Black NBA players are clearly much more often portrayed as successful because of natural physical abilities and that this must leave a deep impression on children, particularly when communities are segregated, and community members do not have the opportunity to play with athletes from other ethnic origins.

It is not surprising that many youngsters are tempted into sports when they witness the success of their idols through the media. LeBron James earns over US$20 million per year from his salary alone. The myth of meritocracy is clearly perpetuated in his life story. He was born in 1984 in Akron, Ohio to a 16-year-old mother, Gloria Marie James. He lived in the poorest neighborhoods of Akron until his mother found a more stable lifestyle for him with Frank Walker, a local youth football coach. The ideology of sports as a level playing field for all members of society, and the concept that an athlete's success is proportional to hard work, are clearly legitimised through these individual cases. Chenoweth (1974) further explains that when athletes are seen to succeed in this way through hard work, they are promoting stability in society as others will also strive to achieve. Those who fail are more likely to consider their own shortcomings rather than the unfairness of the system itself. Thus, as Harper et al. (2013) state 'widespread inequities are cyclically reproduced' and the sport industry maintains its flow of elite athletes to perpetuate the system. In reality, the kind of success in sports that LeBron James represents is extremely rare and only involves a very small percentage of the athletes who strive for success. Merely 0.03% of high school players go on to be professionals in the NBA. However, despite this, these fashionable and popular sports icons are continuously presented, and the media attention resonates within the community, maintaining a very high level of competition within the sport, and a strong desire to achieve success.

Moreover, only Black African Americans who subscribe to this system are successful. This is clearly demonstrated in the way that Colin Kaepernick has been treated due to his political convictions. His protest led to his end at the NFL. The message to aspiring athletes is to not mix their athletics with politics. Kaepernick proclaimed about the injustice of several police shootings in the summer of 2016 leading up to the 2016-2017 NFL season:

> "I am not going to stand up to show pride in a flag for a country that oppresses Black people and people of color...To me this is bigger than football and it would be selfish on my part to look the other way" (Hauser, 2016).

The protest developed into a social movement with other players taking a knee during the anthem. In September 2016, Kaepernick's protest was joined by Brandon Marshall of the Denver Broncos. That month of September, 2016, saw the Colin Kaepernick Effect take flight. The protests developed to high school players. It occurred at Brunswick High in Ohio, Castlemont School in Oakland, California, Withrow High School in Cincinnati, at the Victory & Praise Christian Academy football team and in others across the US. In September 2017, Principal Waylon Bates of Parkway High School in Louisiana labelled the movement a 'disruption' (Bogage, 2017). Evidently, this became a much more serious issue at this stage because high schools are the breeding grounds for professional athletes. Thus, social activism in these contexts might mean that political athletes were being socialised into sport. This was a serious issue for the white establishment and must be one of the main causes of the harshness of the treatment Kaepernick has subdued. No NFL teams are prepared to hire him.

Currently in 2018, there is some research that argues that there is no 'implicit bias' in police officers towards minorities (Cesario, 2018); that they only shoot at violent crime scenes specifically if their assailant is armed. It appears that these cases are heavilly populated by Blacks, hence the larger number of Black shootings. Notwithstanding the reasons behind the high number, the fact is that Black Americans account for 30% of people fatally shot by police despite making up 13% of the population (Cesario, 2018). Kaepernick reacted and launched a campaign in a response to these numbers.

Film is also a medium for the propagation of this phenomenon. Altman (1984) argues that films play a part in propagating 'color blindness'. As Boyle (2009) testifies 'mediated discourses of sport play an important part in reproducing, naturalizing and even constructing values, attitudes, and sometimes prejudices' (p. 15). The film, *The Blind Side* was tremendously successful. It cost $29 million to produce but brought in $250 million at the box office in the US and $309 million globally. It also raised $102 million in DVD sales (Montez de Oca, 2012). Sandra Bullock won an Academy Award as Best Actress and a Golden Globe Award (Boyle, 2009). In the Blind Side (2009), the African American footballer, Michael Oher, struggles academically. The white American character Leigh Anne Tuohy (Oher's white adoptive mother), played by Sandra Bullock, is determined to help him. This Christian generosity is for Bonilla-Silva (2014), a characteristic of the paradox of race or 'racism without racists'. In other words, Sandra Bullock's white supremacy enables her to feel qualified to help Oher. This power she depicts has been described as presenting 'white saviour syndrome' (Cammarota, 2011, p. 242). As Cammarota (2011) states:

> 'White saviour syndrome has the tendency to render people of colour incapable of helping themselves—infantile or hapless/helpless victims who survive by instinct' (p. 242).

It is the Whites who are portrayed as the gatekeepers to success. Similarly, in a film documentary such as *Hoop Dreams*, African American children are inspired that it is through the help of a white gatekeeper that they could ascend out of poverty. These films reinforce the attachment to this ideal. This is a common element to sport films with African Americans. Its power is described by journalist Melissa Anderson (2009):

> 'The movie peddles the most insidious kind of racism, one in which whiteys are virtuous saviours, coming to the rescue of Blacks who become superfluous in narratives that are supposed to be about them' http://www.dallasobserver.com/film/the-blind-side-what-would-black-people-do-without-nice-white-folks-6420117.

The focus on saving seeks to 'soften the power of the oppressor in deference to the weakness of the oppressed' (Freire, 1998, p. 46). From an Althusserian reading, it is clear that the African Americans in the films discussed do not have the agency required to make any change (Althusser & Balibar, 1979). They are hailed to seek recognition and help from whites. Oher himself reported this. It was presented in several newspapers, including the *Baltimore Sun* after he had successfully won the Super Bowl with the Baltimore Ravens, in 2013:

> 'I'm tired of the movie. Football is what got me here, and the movie, it wasn't me. Sports is all I had growing up, and the movie made me look like I didn't know anything' (Wilson, 2013). http://www.baltimoresun.com/sports/ravens/ravens-insider/bal-michael-oher-tired-of-hearing-about-blind-side-movie-20130129-story.html

Here, he distinctly refers to his presentation as an agent without agency depicted as a naïve dependent. Additionally, in films like *The Blind Side*, the social and economic problems inherent in society such as unemployment and crime impacting Black communities are not discussed. Blacks are socialised out of discussing such issues.

This lack of agency is seen in films such as *Gladiator* (2000) and *Million Dollar Baby* in which the African American is consistently in a secondary role to a White protagonist (Baker, 2003). Playing a minor role in a sport film is another archetypal feature of the subtlety of racist ideology. *Gladiator* (2000), a film awarded five Oscars, exemplifies this. It celebrates the white protagonist's adventure with a Black compatriot playing a supportive role. The Black and White partnerships are portrayed as harmonious, but this is only so because there is hierarchy already embedded in the relationship.

In contrast to African Americans, Whites in sport and sport films, are viewed as being better at leadership and teamwork. If White NBA players are portrayed as successful, it is because of hard work and intelligence, not natural ability (Goss et al. 2010). Whites are perceived as having only a 'modest athletic endowment' (Harris, 2000, p.69). This leads to the establishment of the phenomenon of 'stacking'. As Giulianotti (2005) observes:

> 'Stacking is defined as the placement of white athletes in central positions associated with intelligence, decision making, leadership, calmness and dependability. And the location of non-whites in peripheral positions requiring explosive physical powers' (p. 74).

Stacking is evident in films such as *The Longest Yard*. It is interesting to note that the original film in 1974 with Burt Reynolds as the prisoner/quarterback had a primarily white population. This has been significantly changed for the second version; the players in the American football team are primarily Black. However, in this 2005 version, it is the white Adam Sandler who plays Paul Crewe the professional quarterback forced to form a team in prison to play the guards. He is presented as the white hope; coach and leader for the Black athletes. It is also the white Reynolds who provides advice to Sandler. This socialises Blacks into viewing themselves as subordinate, and whites as superior.

There are very few analyses of Blacks in leadership positions in sport films. However, one such film in which an African American holds a leadership role is *Remember the Titans* (2000). This is chosen for a critical race theory (CRT) analysis by Cranmer and Harris (2015). Cranmer and Harris (2015) state: 'This film is unique in the sport film genre because it explicitly focuses on issues of racism, interracial interactions, and leadership' (p. 156). It was made by Gregory Allen Howard with the 'purpose of advancing the cause of social justice by producing a film that could potentially become an exemplar of interracial cohesion' (Cranmer & Harris, 2015, p. 166). However, Cranmer and Harris (2015) are very critical of this film despite its wishful advocacy stance. Herman Boone (Denzel Washington), head coach of the T. C. Williams football team, replaces Yoast (Will Patton), a successful White coach who has won the season 15 times. Cranmer and Harris (2015) write that hiring Boone appears to be a progressive move yet they explain how this selection reveals 'subversive and selfish motives of a White system and exposes a specific set of circumstances where Black leadership is deemed acceptable' (p. 158). Boone must face systematic challenges from the White institutions; for example, he is threatened with the sack if the team loses one game. Additionally, his position of authority is undermined by white subordinates. Racial stacking of leadership positions among players is also evident. The team captain and quarterback are both white and take decisions without Boone's knowledge or approval. In sum, despite its claims of presenting an African American in a leadership role, the reality of that status is undermined in several ways. That said, the authors do conclude that by using CRT as a lens, audiences can be shown how to critically assess the embedded meanings in the visual text to be empowered to consider issues of social justice and equality (Orbe & Kinefuchi, 2008; Yosso, 2002). In theory, this is indeed a sound point but without the educational background, it might not be possible for a wider audience to conduct this kind of deconstruction. Consequently, there is inherent socializing power in the film.

This sort of stacking in films helps to justify its reality in sport and this is reflected back into media providing a strong symbiotic relationship between the two. Lomax (2008) reports on research stating that the number of Blacks in positions of authority is extremely low. In the NBA and NFL, Beamon and Messner (2014) state coaching, leadership and management positions are almost exclusively occupied by Whites' (p. 184). Cunningham and Bopp (2010) conclude their research into hiring processes in the NFL by declaring that Whites are more usually hired in coordinating positions and that 'Whites were more likely than African Americans to be depicted as helping the team through their knowledge and experience' (p. 1). Further, in an article by Woodward (2004), scouts for the annual National Football League amateur draft were examined and were found to inherently focus on the African American players in physical terms and the White players in the same positions were often discussed in relation to their intellect and decision-making capabilities. Similarly, NCAA sports have a low percentage of Black administrators and coaches in comparison to the number of Black athletes involved in playing the sports. Stacking is also present in other areas of sport. Anderson (1993) demonstrates from data compiled from 85 NCAA division 1-A institutions, that athletic directors, head football coaches, and full time assistant football coaches are most commonly whites. He concludes that these data prove that 'career opportunity is restricted for Blacks by institutionalised discrimination in intercollegiate sport' (p. 61). This also relates to the occupational segregation on the baseball playing field that Sack et al. (2005) present from their research. These authors found that stacking persists in Major League Baseball. Blacks are less likely to be assigned to thinking roles such as the pitcher position than other roles where physical characteristics such as speed and power hitting are more important. These characteristics help to form thinking acting as socialising forces.

It is clear that racial ideologies, which act as socialising agents in the sporting environment, are prominent. These are seen in the socialising agents in American society. As Beamon (2010) and Beamon and Messner (2014) have shown, it appears for African Americans that professional athletics is a feasible career path and that barriers to success are low. However, there is little opportunity to do this, in reality. In fact, Giulianotti (2005) cites LaFeber who claims that only 1 in 135, 800 athletes will become part of the NBA (p. 73). As Beamon and Messner (2014) state, statistically it is easier for an African-American male to become a neurosurgeon than a player in the NBA. Additionally, in their research, Beamon and Messner (2014) present how NFL and NBA athletes reveal that they feel that they have no control over their lives and that they are owned by the team (p. 186). It is a truism that no contract is legitimately guaranteed, and a player may be traded or taken out of the squad at any time (Beamon and Messner, 2014, p. 186). In the same research, the authors also present how several athletes perceive 'disrespect' from white coaches and management.

Three primary arguments have been made in this chapter regarding the socialising processes of African Americans into sport. The first is that African Americans consistently face access discrimination to education and are led to believe, through significant peers in the neighbourhood where they are born, that there is a way out of poverty through sport (Beamon, 2010). The second is that the proportion of African Americans hired in management roles is significantly lower than the proportion of African American athletes present in professional sport (Beamon & Messner, 2014). Therefore, athletes are socialised into non-management roles making them dependent on Whites for their successes. Finally, the media and film have a very active role in perpetuating the racial ideology dominant in American society (Altman, 1984; Boyle, 2009; Cranmer & Harris, 2015). This helps to maintain myths about differences between White and Black, particularly, the notion that the white can achieve success through hard work and intelligence whereas the Black athlete has a natural talent for power and speed.

Collectively, these findings demonstrate that Whites enjoy privileged positions both in and outside of sport. Clearly, structural and ideological transformation must occur to make inroads into changing this situation. Cunningham and Bopp (2010) argue that it is necessary that more African Americans hold positions of power within organisations and that training and educational efforts are made to develop their skills. They refer to Parks and Roberton's (2002) findings demonstrating that training efforts of this type may result in a more meaningfully inclusive structure. At the same time, Cunningham and Bopp (2010) posit that these institutionally constructed practices and norms need to be represented in media releases. Press releases and the production of films that do not perpetuate the dominant racial ideology need to be aired in a consistent way and on a wide scale. However, these same authors also admit that the structures of racism are very much deep-seated and that changes can only occur through substantial socio-economic change.

Beamon and Messner (2014) conclude that while it may seem counterintuitive for the media to present more of the stories of African Americans as 'losers', as the film *Hoop Dreams* ultimately does, this is a more accurate and informative depiction of the reality for the majority. Without this honesty, sport remains an area of abnormally contested terrain. Beamon and Messner (2014) argue that it should not at least be viewed as an easy way to become successful and pull oneself and one's family out of poverty. Although rare, there are occasionally films that have sought to reveal Blacks in dominant leadership roles in sport, such as *Remember the Titans* (2000). This has perhaps enabled audiences to see how powerful socialisation processes are and how difficult access can be.

In conclusion, racism is maintained through a complex nexus constructed of various ideological means, one of which is the argument that Black African Americans are more naturally predisposed to sporting excellence. Others include media and film, and this influences primary agents who hold beliefs that a career in sport is achievable. This is a result of racial stacking. Sport is therefore used as an ideological socialising tool for political means. However, when it is used as this tool against the White establishment, there is outcry. There have been several other cases of Black civil rights movements in sports, some of which history takes pride in valuing much later on, notably the Black Power salute from Tommie Smith and John Carlos at the 1968 Olympics, and Muhammed Ali's refusal to go to Vietnam in 1967 (Calamur, 2016). Whites have also participated in these movements. One notable case are the boycotts of South African sport during the Apartheid era. For this latter, when Apartheid was dismantled, sports lifted the boycotts and South Africa was readmitted into the International sports federations. For the Black population, if oppression is present, sport is one of the main avenues to express discontent as it is an environment populated by successful Blacks. It is, in these cases, a diplomatic tool and a way to avoid violent protest. Kaepernick's peaceful protest is a part of the Black historical narrative and it seemed, to some extent, to be tolerated until the high schools became involved. When that occurred, it became too widespread, and a potentially dangerous, civil rights movement. However, the establishment has not completely sidelined the take-a-knee campaign. Despite his ostracism, Kaepernick is one of Nike's 'Just Do It' ad campaign representatives (Bonds-Staples, 2018). He has also been awarded Sports Illustrated's Muhammad Ali Legacy Award. This demonstrates that, even in the establishment, many will support a just cause and a peaceful protest.

REFERENCES

Althusser, L. and Balibar, E. (1979). "Reading Capital". London: NLB.

Altman, R. (1984). "A semantic/syntactic approach to film genre". *Cinema Journal*, 6-18.

Anderson, D. (1993). "Cultural diversity on campus: A look at intercollegiate football coaches". *Journal of Sport and Social Issues*, *17*(1), 61-66.

Baker, A. (2003). *Contesting identities: Sports in American film*. University of Illinois Press.

Bandura, A. (1963). *Social learning and personality development*. New York: Holt, Rinehart, and Winston.

Beamon, K. K. (2008). "Used Goods: Former African American College Student-Athletes' Perception of Exploitation by Division I Universities". *The Journal of Negro Education*, 352-364.

———. (2010) "Are Sports Overemphasized in the Socialization Process of African American Males? A Qualitative Analysis of Former Collegiate Athletes' Perception of Sport Socialization". *Journal of Black Studies, 41(2)*, 281–300.

Beamon, K., & Messer, C. (2014). "Professional sports experiences as contested racial terrain". *Journal of African American Studies*, *18*(2), 181-191.

Bogage, J. (2017). Louisiana high school will kick students off team if they don't stand for national anthem. *Washington Post*. Retrieved in November 2018 from https://www.washingtonpost.com/news/early-lead/wp/2017/09/28/louisiana-high-school-will-kick-students-off-team-if-they-dont-stand-for-national-anthem/?utm_term=.e72c28caf67b

Bonds-Staples,G. (2018). This Life: If Nike can stand with Kaepernick, I can shell out extra for sneakers. *The Atlanta Journal-Constitution*. Retrieved in November, 2018 from https://www.ajc.com/lifestyles/nike-can-stand-with-kaepernick-can-shell-out-extra-for-sneakers/5VwzXuT2oLlK1vObmgjGMP/

Bonilla-Silva, E. (2014). *Racism without racists: Colour-blind racism and racial inequality in contemporary America* (4th ed.). Lanham: Rowman & Littlefield Publishers.

Boyle, R. (2009). *Power Play: Sport, the Media and Popular Culture: Sport, the Media and Popular Culture*. Edinburgh University Press.

Brooks, S. N., & McKail, M. A. (2008). "A theory of the preferred worker: A structural explanation for black male dominance in basketball". *Critical Sociology, 34*(3), 369-387.

Calamur, K. (2016) Muhammad Ali and Vietnam. His refusal to be drafted to fight in the war transcended the boxing ring, which he had dominated, at great personal cost. The Atlantic. retrieved in

November, 2018 from https://www.theatlantic.com/news/archive/2016/06/muhammad-ali-vietnam/485717/

Cammarota, J. (2011). Blindsided by the Avatar: White Saviors and Allies Out of Hollywood and in Education, *Review of Education, Pedagogy, and Cultural Studies*, 33 (3), 242-259.

Cesario, J. (2018). A new look at racial disparities in police use of deadly force. *The Conversation*. Retrieved November, 2018 from http://theconversation.com/a-new-look-at-racial-disparities-in-police-use-of-deadly-force-98681

Champagne, F. (2009). "Beyond nature vs. nurture: Philosophical insights from molecular biology". *APS Observer*, 22 (4), pp. 1-3.

Chenoweth, L. (1974). *The American dream of success: The search for the self in the twentieth century*. Brooks/Cole.

Copeland, T. R. (2017). Athletic Disobedience: Providing a Context for Analysis of Colin Kaepernick's Protest, Fair Play. *Revista de Filosofía, Ética y Derecho del Deporte*, 10C, 84-107.

Cranmer, G. A., & Harris, T. M. (2015). "White-Side, Strong-Side: A Critical Examination of Race and Leadership in Remember the Titans". *Howard Journal of Communications*, 26(2), 153-171.

Cunningham, G. B., & Bopp, T. (2010). "Race ideology perpetuated: Media representations of newly hired football coaches". *Journal of Sports Media*, 5(1), 1-19.

Delpit, L. (2012). *Multiplication is for White people: Raising expectations for other people's children*. New York: The New Press.

Edwards, H. (2000). "Crisis of Black athletes on the eve of the 21st century". *Society, 37*, 9–13.

Entine, J. (2012). *The DNA Olympics Jamaicans Win Sprinting 'Genetic Lottery' and Why We Should All Care*. [online] Retrieved from: http://www.forbes.com/sites/jonentine/2012/08/12/the -dna-olympics-jamaicans-win-sprinting-geneticlottery-and-why-we-should-all-care/3

Entine, J. (2000). *Taboo. Why black athletes dominate sports & why we're afraid to talk about it*. New York: Public Affairs.

ESPN News Service: http://www.espn.com/nfl/story/_/id/21682144/beyonce-presents-colin-kaepernick-sports-illustrated-muhammad-ali-legacy-award).

Eynon, N., Ruiz, J. R., Oliveira, J., Duarte, J. A., Birk, R., & Lucia, A. (2011). "Genes and elite athletes: a roadmap for future research". *The Journal of physiology*, 589(13), 3063-3070.

Freire, P. (1998). *Pedagogy of freedom: Ethics, democracy, and civic courage*. Rowman & Littlefield.

Giulianotti, R. (2005). *Sport: A critical sociology*. Polity Press: Cambridge.

Goss, B. D., Tyler, A. L., & Billings, A. C. (2009). "A content analysis of racial representations of NBA athletes on Sports Illustrated magazine covers", 1970-2003. In H.L Hundley & A. C. Billings (Eds.), *Examining Identity in Sports Media* (pp. 173-195). Thousand Oaks, CA: Sage Publications, Inc.

Harper, S. R., Williams Jr, C. D., & Blackman, H. W. (2013). "Black male student-athletes and racial inequities in NCAA Division I college sports". *Center for the Study of Race & Equity in Education*.

Harris, O. (1994). "Race, sport, and social support". *Sociology of Sport Journal, 11*, 40–50

———. (2000). "African-American predominance in college sport". In D. Brooks & R. Althouse (Eds.), *Racism in college sport: The African American athlete's experience (pp. 51–74)*. Morgantown, WV: Fitness Information Technology.

Hauser, C. (2016). Ruth Bader Ginsburg Calls Colin Kaepernick's National Anthem Protest 'Dumb'. Retrieved on November 21 2016 from http://www.nytimes.com/2016/10/12/us/ruthbader-ginsburg-calls-colin-kaepernicks-national-anthem-protest-dumb.html Hauser.

Herrnstein, R., & Murray, C. (1994). *The Bell Curve*. New York: Free Press.

Hoberman, J. M. (1977). "Sport and political ideology". *Journal of sport and social issues*, 1(2), 80-114.

Hoberman, J. M. (1997). *Darwin's athletes: How sport has damaged Black America and preserved the myth of race*. Houghton Mifflin Harcourt.

Hylton, K. (2009). *'Race' and sport: Critical race theory*. London: Routledge.

Jacobs, P. (2015, January 27). *Here's the Insane Amount of Time Student-Athletes Spend on Practice.* Retrieved from http://www.businessinsider.com/college-student-athletes-spend-40-hours-a-week-practicing-2015-1

Lapchick, R. (2011) *Racial and gender report card.* Retrieved from http://web.bus.ucf.edu/sportbusiness/?page=1445.

Lomax, M. E. (2008). *Sports and the Racial Divide: African American and Latino Experience in an Era of Change.* Jackson, Mississippi: University Press of Mississippi.

Lyall, S. (2014). U.N.C. "Investigation Reveals Athletes Took Fake Classes". *The New York Times.* Retrieved from https://www.nytimes.com/2014/10/23/sports/university-of-north-carolina-investigation-reveals-shadow-curriculum-to-help-athletes.html

Montez de Oca, J. (2012). "White domestic goddess on a postmodern plantation: Charity and commodity racism in The Blind Side". *Sociology of Sport Journal, 29,* 131–150.

Nixon, Howard L. (1984). *Sport, society, and the American dream.* Leisure Press: NY.

Omi, M., & Winant, H. (1986). *Racial formation in the United States: From the 1960s to the 1980s.* New York: Routledge.

Orbe, M. P., & Kinefuchi, E. (2008). "Crash under investigation: Engaging complications of complicity, coherence, and implicature through critical analysis". *Critical Studies in Media Communication, 25,* 135–156.

Parks, J. B., & Roberton, M. A. (2002). "The gender gap in student attitudes toward sexist/nonsexist language: Implications for sport management education". *Journal of Sport Management, 16,* 190–208.

Plaschke, B. (2013, February 1). "Michael Oher prefers his Super Bowl role to being in Blind Side". *Los Angeles Times.* Retrieved from http://articles.latimes.com/2013/feb/01/sports/la-sp-plaschke-super-bowl-oher-20130201.

Sack, A. L., Singh, P., & Thiel, R. (2005). "Occupational segregation on the playing field: The case of Major League Baseball". *Journal of Sport Management, 19,* 300–318.

Thurtle, P. (2007). *The emergence of genetic rationality.* Seattle: University of Washington Press.

Woodward, J. R. (2004). "Professional football scouts: An investigation of racial stacking". *Sociology of sport journal, 21*(4), 356-375.

Yang, N., MacArthur, D. G., Gulbin, J. P., Hahn, A. G., Beggs, A. H., Easteal, S., & North, K. (2003). "ACTN3 genotype is associated with human elite athletic performance". *The American Journal of human genetics, 73*(3), 627-631.

Yosso, T. J. (2002). "Critical race media literacy: Challenging deficit discourse about Chicanas/os". *Journal of Popular Film & Television, 30,* 52–62.

CHAPTER 4

Corporate Sports Socialisation and Habitus: Adventure Racing and Dragon Boating

Sport and workplace culture can be seen to have a long history particularly in Scandinavian countries and socialist regimes. Employees are socialised into sport for bonding, fitness and focus. Today, it is present as a global phenomenon with branding events such as the Standard Chartered Marathon. Indeed, as the link has developed, it has become popular to posit that soft skills learned from sport transfer to the workplace. For example, in their well-known book, *Applied Sport Management Skills*, Lussier and Kimball (2014) link organisational culture with team sport culture. They state that the ideal in both is to develop bonds to build a solid group identity. This argument is taken up in many other sources. However, only a few have analysed the notion of value engineering as a motivation for socialisation into a corporate sport (Lyng, 1990; Fletcher, 2008; Kay & Laberge, 2002). Most academic studies on corporate sport do not tend to explore this relationship. Instead, they have concentrated more on Corporate Social Responsibility (CSR).

In this chapter, research relating to corporate culture and sport is explored. The main case studies, analysed in depth, relate to adventure racing as well as dragon boating. However, at the end of the chapter, an analysis of potential research on golf and tennis culture is also provided. Very little research exists in this field yet it is one with a great deal of scope that could provide interesting findings. The two case studies on adventure racing and dragon boating examine whether the reasons for socialisation into these sports are similar at the structural and agency levels. That is, whether the corporate discourse is similar to the individual discourses reported through research in this field. Commonly, the corporate discourse presents, even mythologises, the synchronisation learned through effort, teamwork and collective goal-seeking to increase performativity. However, it is not sure that the discourse is the same at the individual level. Human agents involved in the sport may be socialised into participating for reasons contrary to the corporate objectives behind the setting up of the sporting practice; for example, to relax from work or build friendships outside of corporate culture. Consequently, the tensions between structure and agency in this field could be very interesting.

Eichberg (2009) writes that:

> 'Hierarchy is, indeed, a central feature of the 'organic' corporative idea. In contrast, the principle of cooperation is based on activity and self-determination from below. It represents workplace democracy. Company sport is a part of this game' (p. 167).

Eichberg (2009) has noted how sport is an effective way to empower participants from below as it enables relationships across potential workplace boundaries to be transcended. This has been an important goal in Nordic countries. Developing 'workplace democracy' with systems in which cooperation and corporation can co-exist has long been sought after. Today, this democratic view of the workplace has grown on a much greater scale to be a part of new corporate management culture. Notions of empowerment for all employees is reflected in much of the modern-day management discourse. For example, it is core to Wilkinson's (1998) Theory of Empowerment in the Workplace, a well-known work focused on making changes in traditional corporate management, and one which is used as an analytical tool in this chapter in the section on dragon boating.

The argument that socialising employees into corporate sport culture may help to develop cooperation within the corporate structure and facilitate workplace democracy tends to be very common in the corporate discourse around certain modes of sport participation. This has led to research projects such as Kay and Laberge's (2002) examination of corporate agents' participation in adventure racing and Brooke's (2015) analysis of corporate dragon boating. These studies set out to explore whether it is true that individuals participate in corporate sport to develop unity and if so, how successful they perceive it to be in facilitating new corporate culture related to empowerment. In other words, through qualitative interviews with participants, these authors have sought to find out why individuals participate in these sports and if these reasons are the same as, or in contradiction to, the corporate reasoning behind socialising these agents into the sporting practice.

Corporate Adventure racing started out in New Zealand and then grew to be popular in Europe two decades ago. The pinnacle of its development was observed in the extremely popular Eco-Challenge launched by Mark Burnett and partnered with Discovery Channel in 1996. It presents teams of 4 of mixed gender engaging in expedition-length 24 hour a day races over 300-miles, in differing locations around the world requiring athletes to risk injury and weight loss, and contest with extreme weather, harsh terrain and sleep deprivation. Contests involved a variety of disciplines such as canoeing, camel or horse-riding, mountaineering, mountain biking, scuba diving and trekking. The Discovery Channel Eco-Challenge (DCEC) is generally considered to be one of the first examples of reality showing, also known as 'dramalities'.

In their study, the 'New' Corporate Habitus in Adventure Racing published in the *International Review for the Sociology of Sport*, Kay and Laberge (2002) explain how 61% of DCEC contestants are corporate management agents. These participants cite AR as their preferred sport. They also describe their workplace belonging to 'new' corporate cultures. Kay and Laberge (2002) contrast these athletes with AR professionals, who make up around 11% of the contestant population. These others tend to be involved for economic gain from prizes and sponsorship as well as cultural capital linked to competitive rankings. Kay and Laberge (2002) wanted to find out, through qualitative means, corporate agents' primary motivations for participation and whether their DCEC experience provided a 'transferable learning opportunity' (p. 7). Adventure Racing (AR) of this genre might therefore be said to have a status as a symbolic practice if its advocates claim that by participating in it, transferable learning from one context to another can occur. If this is true, this socialisation mechanism is an effective one for corporations.

Kay and Laberge (2002) conduct multiple modes of data generation. They do a media analysis of Discovery Channel Eco-Challenge broadcasts from 1996 to 1999. They also interview 37 contestants, of which 30 occurred during a 3-week Eco-challenge competition. They then follow-up with a further 20 interviews with participants to expand on responses. Additionally, one of the authors competed in a 36-hour race in Quebec to better enable her to relate to the athletes and provide an insider perspective on the races. They (2002) explain the motivation for this approach:

> 'Our goal was to maintain an integrated approach that follows in the ethnographic tradition which rejects positivist views of scientific research' (p. 20).

Following a sociological reflexivity, the authors sought to provide an in-depth understanding of the practices and dispositions of the participants.

Kay and Laberge (2002) apply Bourdieu's (1986) notion of *'habitus'* to describe their participants' behaviours and choices. This helps to understand people's tastes and dispositions towards certain values and activities including sporting preference. With regard to dispositions related to sport, Bourdieu (1986) states that:

> 'To understand the class distribution of the various sports, one would have to take account of the representations which, in terms of their specific schemes of perception and appreciation, the different classes have of the costs (economic, cultural and 'physical') and benefits attached to the different sports—immediate or deferred 'physical' benefits (health, beauty, strength, whether visible, through 'body-building' or invisible through 'keep-fit' exercises), economic and social benefits (upward mobility etc.) immediate or deferred symbolic benefits linked to the distributional or positional value of each of the sports considered[...], gains in distinction accruing from the different effects on the body itself (e.g. slimness, sun-tan, muscles obviously or discreetly visible, etc.) or from the access to highly selective groups which some of these sports give (golf, polo etc.)' (p. 20).

Thus, *habitus* is an effective concept for analysing why people take up certain sport practices and exist in these as social spaces. It allows the researcher to see how these relate to an individual's disposition.

In their findings from interviews, Kay and Laberge (2002) highlight that, in the beginning, participation in AR was largely due to the emergence of a 'new' corporate discourse encouraging a flatter rather than hierarchical organisational structure. This was seen as a moving away from the traditional corporate culture. However, these authors find that once the AR culture had developed, and employees continued in their participation in this field, individual benefits for hedonistic reasons, such as testing their personal limits, rather than collective benefits, took over as the principle motivators. According to Kay and Laberge (2002), these returns are linked to a 'morality of pleasure' or 'hedonistic project' (Kay and Laberge, 2002, p.26). Continued socialisation into the sport was also reported to be for developing cultural capital. Participants reported that they participated in the sport to build their individual status in the corporate ranks. Kay and Laberge (2002) posit:

> 'We have shown that a majority of these participants see or present AR as primarily a self-actualization and management exercise' (p. 31).

Consequently, once the field had emerged into a popular one, socialisation into, and continuation in, the AR culture was more for competitive values; those which helped participants to stand out among their social group. In this way, AR acted as an important social signifier for individual status. The result was therefore contrary to the original new corporate ideals of promoting a democratic, flatter structure. It seems that hierarchy was still very important to these participants.

In this section, the corporate culture of dragon boating in South East Asia is explored and particularly the reasons behind members' participation and whether these are the same as the corporation's objectives. Dragon boating attracts a great deal of interest with South East Asian corporates because it is connected to ancient Asian culture and mythology; but more importantly, because of the discourse provided about the need for synchronisation in the boat, learned through effort, teamwork and collective goal-seeking to increase performativity. Socialisation into this corporate sport is focused on the metaphorical significance it has linked to a corporation as a 'tightly-run ship'.

Dragon boating competitions have existed since ancient Olympia in Southern China. Each year, in many cities and towns across Asia, there is a Dragon Boat Festival, also known as Duanwu Festival. Differing legends attempt to romanticise the beginning of the sport, but the most common origin is based on Qu Yuan (屈原, 340-278 BC), an official of the Chu State during the Warring States period, and talented poet. The story recounts that he committed suicide by drowning in Miluo River (a branch of the Yangtze) in 278 BC out of duty to his leader when the Chu State invaded his province. The locals were so deeply proud and fond of him that they threw cooked rice balls into the river to prevent the fish from eating his body. This ritual has developed in modern day as fongzi, or glutinous rice wrapped with bamboo leaves, which are still thrown to the river. The boat trips have developed into dragon boating. Other superstitions and traditional activities have also grown from these ancient times and still retain significance today. For example, on the day of the dragon boat festival, carrying a 'fragrant bag' made from colouful silk and embroidered with images of animals, flowers and fruits. It normally contains mixed Chinese herbal medicines to ward off evil spirits and invite happiness.

A standard dragon boat comprises twenty-two crew members, of whom twenty are paddlers. The twenty-first is a steersperson (or Sweep), looking out the bow side; and the twenty-second is a Drummer, who faces the Paddlers. The Drummer's role is to establish the stroke. The first pair of paddlers are the Strokes. They follow the drum beat for the strokes and the paddlers behind, emulate them. For synchronisation of the paddles touching the water, the paddlers need to base their strokes on the beat of the drum, not the pair in front of them. If so, the boat moves much more quickly. The culture of dragon boating can be seen to relate to new corporate culture for several reasons, not least this focus on synchronisation. Brooke (2015) sought to explore whether this was evident in corporations. His study looks at South East Asia and particularly the reasons behind members' socialisation into corporate dragon boating and whether these are the same as the corporation's objectives.

Eichberg (2009) and the focus on a new cultural model rejecting traditional models of management with very prominent divisions of labour has been discussed in terms of AR and how, as a sporting activity, these notions might be facilitated. Contrary to popular corporate ideology, Kay and Laberge (2002) found that individualistic tendencies were more prominent than collective ones from this pursuit. Brooke (2015) has also contributed in this field, specifically to discern whether, and to what extent, dragon boating might develop corporate dispositions. This he does by analysing data from qualitative interviews for signs of Wilkinson's (1998) Theory of Empowerment related to constructing new corporate culture. Wilkinson (1998) states:

> 'Empowerment is regarded as providing a solution to the age-old problem of Taylorised and bureaucratic workplaces where creativity is stifled, and workers become alienated, showing discontent through individual or collective means' (p. 40).

For Wilkinson (1998), it is empowerment that is key to decreasing dysfunctional systems of control and promoting 'workplace democracy'. This empowerment can be facilitated through five elements: *information sharing; upward problem solving; task autonomy; attitudinal shaping*; and *self-management. Information sharing* is communication from the top down but also from the bottom up. *Upward problem solving* is the right of employees to deal with issues related to the organisation. *Task autonomy* means that employees should have decision-making prerogatives regarding operations. *Attitudinal shaping* refers to developing a feeling of belonging to the company. Finally, *self-management* refers to providing employees with greater activity in business decisions.

Dragon boating has a strong hold in corporate practice in South East Asia. For example, the Singapore Dragon Boat Association (SDBA) comprises over 100 affiliates, many of which are corporate teams such as Cosmos Tpc; DBS Asia Dragons; Deloitte & Touche LLP; ExxonMobil; EY; GECOKs; Hewlett Packard Asia Pacific; Hewlett Packard Singapore; Keppel Dragons; Marina Bay Sands Dragons; PCS Spitfire; POSB Dragons; PwC; SingHealth Services; Standard Chartered Bank; Team OCBC Dragons. Events are also named after corporations. One of the main ones of the year is the DBS Marina Regatta. The event operators sector is also developed today with some organisations like SAVA and Dragon Boat Innovate (DBI) specialising in corporate dragon boating by selling hiring dragon boats as well as coaching paddlers.

SAVA and Dragon Boat Innovate (DBI) sell dragon boating as a 'unique platform' to attract clients. Firstly, they argue that it is important to keep the Asian cultural heritage alive. Secondly, they point out that it is as an excellent '*ice-breaker*', '*motivational activity*'; and '*teambuilding exercise*'. Brooke (2015) cites several other references to data in the promotional material that makes these same points (http://www.youtube.com/watch?v=7X5a_4zoS_I#t=198). However, some distinctions are made. In a comparison between the workplace and the dragon boat community, the former is said to comprise a group of individuals but in the latter, a single unit:

> 'When you're on the boat, everything's just outside the boat. You become friends with each other…you are a team; where here (at work), even if I work in a team, you see a lot of individuals in a team, more (like) a blend' (p. 105)

The discourse focuses on how teamwork building through dragon boating socialisation can enhance corporate performance. This is further explained from a DBI promotional video. Through dragon boating, paddlers learn important corporate notions such as '*focus*' and '*alignment*'.

> 'You do not actually see how critical it is. But when you're in the boat, the slightest misalignment, and uh, it's the difference between winning and losing' (p. 106).

Brooke (2015) presents how dragon boat specialist companies sell the activity for socialisation purposes based on high performativity. A SAVA employee states:

> 'We also highlight that synchronizing is what really makes a difference, like a team with lesser strength but better synchronization can actually be a stronger team right? So, at the same way that their workplace, teams that are in sync and have good communication within their members, they also can achieve their organizational goals' (p. 106).

The message here is that even a smaller company, with fewer financial resources, may succeed if it builds these key notions of unity, focus and alignment. Further, a successful dragon boating team is said to be excellent for '*brand building*' with a strong image advertised at events. Additionally, there is a discourse related to less prominent managerial demarcations compared to the corporate past. In the dragon boat, there is a necessary lack of social status; the boat brings staff '*from CEO to janitor together to achieve a common goal*' (DBI video) and each has equal importance. Finally, dragon boating can lead to '*boosting employee self-confidence and motivation*'; '*developing physical health*' and '*destressing*'. According to SAVA (http://www.sava.com.sg/), the gains from socialising employees into the activity might lead to '*increased productivity and effectiveness*' and '*decreased absenteeism*'.

Having collected data from an interview with a corporate dragon boat participant, Brooke (2015) establishes three selective codes from the data that help to determine the motivations for socialisation of employees into the corporate dragon boat culture.

These are *teamwork and performativity*; *field transformation*; and *identity building and accruing capital*. For the first, *teamwork and performativity*, the interviewee was very positive about other members in the dragon boat team, referring consistently to *friends*. This links to Wilkinson's (1998) theory of positive *attitudinal shaping* within the new ideals for corporate structure. Brooke (2015) also found instances of '*enhanced camaraderie*' by '*putting team before self*" propagating all four of Wilkinson's (1998) Theory of Empowerment elements. Thus, socialisation into the sport does enhance a flatter structure than the traditional one but whether this is transferable is another matter. For the second, *field transformation*, the interviewee explained that dragon boating as a recreation outside work is deeply appreciated. The participant also mentioned the online interactive platform for photos and discussions for members. This allowed, in particular, for *information sharing* and sometimes *upward problem solving*. However, what emerged related to this, is that the associations constructed through dragon boating tended to focus on the recreational association's business, not that of the corporation's. In sum, employees chose their socialisation into the dragon boat culture because it existed as a separate social space in employees' minds, not an extension of the corporation. Brooke (2015) posits that this might be seen to be in opposition to notions of transfer to the workplace setting. For the third, *identity building and accruing capital*, dragon boating is seen as highly meaningful to participants' life-worlds. As with Kay and Laberge (2002), dragon boating participation offers what Bourdieu terms 'social capital'. It helps to construct participant and group identities. Bourdieu (1986) defines 'social capital' as

> 'the aggregate of the actual or potential resources which are linked to possession of a durable network of more or less institutionalized relationships of mutual acquaintance and recognition—or in other words, to membership in a group—which provides each of its members with the backing of the collectivity-owned capital, a 'credential' which entitles them to credit, in the various senses of the word' (p. 248-149).

From this study, socialisation into and continuation in corporate dragon boating acted as a 'credential'. Similarly, to Kay and Laberge's (2002) study, this capital appeared to relate to individual gain and self-actualisation. However, there were also references to the importance of the team in accruing capital for the corporation in the corporate sector. This collectivity might be linked to Confucianism in Asian contexts. Singapore is viewed as a collectivist culture (Lau, 1992) valuing Confucianist ideals (Kuah, 2007); a need for harmony is pervasive (Kuah, 2007). Hence, the relations built around the sport may be more meaningful than the competition at work.

In sum, continued participation in these sports was seen to be for developing cultural capital among a group. However, differences were evident in the studies. For Kay and Laberge's (2002) study, participation in AR was overwhelmingly for self-actualisation whereas, for Brooke (2015), this was also present but being successful in the sport was also seen as a corporate identity marker. In this respect, the capital accrued from the activities leads to a perceived increase in status and this can be seen as empowering for corporate participants, either in individual or group terms.

Additionally, Brooke (2015) concludes that socialisation into dragon boating does enhance a flatter structure than the traditional one but is not sure if there is transferability of this to the workplace. It seemed, from responses, that the solidarity from dragon boating was more related to the social space of the sport rather than the workplace.

As seen in this chapter, corporations value sport, and encourage their members to participate in it. Whether the same values are drawn by the participating individuals is debateable but the corporate motivation is there nonetheless. This can be linked to literature on corporate culture (Deal & Kennedy, 1982; Peters & Waterman, 1982). Deal and Kennedy (1982) state:

> 'Companies that have cultivated their individual identities by shaping values, making heroes, spelling out rites and rituals, and acknowledging the cultural network have an edge. These corporations have values and beliefs to pass along — not just products. They have stories to tell — not just profits to make. They have heroes whom managers and workers can emulate — not just faceless bureaucrats. In short, they are human institutions that provide practical meaning for people, both on and off the job' (p. 15).

Corporate sport can provide a field for this kind of 'practical meaning', or value engineering (Lyng, 1990; Fletcher, 2008; Kay & Laberge, 2002). However, it is not just any sport that is valued. In this chapter, adventure racing and dragon boating have been explored. Future research could also be conducted on other sports. Golf and tennis appear to be the most utilised corporate sports across the globe. Yet there is very little research conducted in this field.

Golf is very popular in North America, where, according to Briassoulis (2010), almost 60% of the world's 32,000 golf courses exist. Twenty percent are in Europe and 12% in Asia. The remaining 8% are in various countries across the globe. In a large-scale quantitative study, utilizing data from a nationally representative survey of US adults, Stempel (2005) found that, in North America, the most class exclusive sport is tennis followed by golf. One of the main reasons why the rich participate in golf, according to Chew (2013) in the Huffington Post, is for the 'legitimacy' it confers its members. It helps to build their identity. The sport has links to ESPN's front page, Rolex and other major brands giving it a high profile. In this way, golf helps to provide the activity for the habitus of the successful corporate individual. Indeed, exclusionary practices are common, and this creates distinction. Distinction exists in the form of membership costs, in particular. In a posting on the site Golfmagic (https://www.golfmagic.com/news/course-news/the-10-most-expensive-golf-club-memberships-in-the-world/14871), a list of the top ten most expensive golf memberships is provided. The second most expensive is Wentworth Golf Club in Surrey, England with an annual fee of £180,000; the first is Liberty National New Jersey, USA at £240,404 or $US306,893.74 annually.

These characteristics have helped to make golf a sport valued by corporations across the globe. An example case study of a company managing corporate golf is ExcusiveGolf. It is based in the UK but operates in 50 countries including North

America. On their front page (https://www.exclusivegolf.co.uk/corporate-golf/), they state:

> 'Why not mix pleasure with business by combining your next corporate event with golf or allow us to organise your complete corporate golf day at home or abroad with meticulous detail and specialist creativity'.

Corporate events such as conferences are intertwined with golfing sessions. Companies can also award their staff with 'stays to play' as recompense for valued work. The frontpage also cites some of its corporate clients: Panasonic, Duetsche Bank, Morgan Stanley, British Gas, Hyundai, Exel and Mitsubishi. Interestingly, a similar internet search for corporate tennis provides organisations such as SelecTennis (http://www.selectennis.com/corporate-clients/), which has a close up photograph, on its page, of a bottle of champagne being poured surrounded by several crystal glasses as its marketing tool. However, companies such as these, marketing to corporations, are much more difficult to find for other sports such as ultimate frisbee or soccer. Indeed, frisbee is clearly marketed as a young, lifestyle sport (Thorpe and Wheaton, 2011a; 2011b), and far from the activities of the corporate executive.

The application of Bourdieu's (1986) notions of field, capital and habitus provides interesting insights into the links between these sports and corporate culture and specifically the way different groups employ them to produce distinctions that act as group identifiers. As Bourdieu (1986) states:

> 'Capital, which, in its objectified or embodied forms, takes time to accumulate and which, as a potential capacity to produce profits and to reproduce itself in identical or expanded form, contains a tendency to persist in its being, is a force inscribed in the objectivity of things so that everything is not equally possible or impossible' (p.241).

Capital is accrued through time and space and different fields have gatekeepers. Golf and tennis can be seen to have significant symbolic benefits for their practitioners linked to their distributional and positional value. Without economic capital, it is difficult to enter into these sports at corporate level. With regards to Bourdieu's notion of cultural capital, once access is attained, golf helps to strengthen its members' 'vision of the world' and 'principles of classification' (Bourdieu, 1999, p. 337). Concerning social capital, these corporate-sponsored sporting activities provide reciprocal acquaintance and identification and enable their select members to construct valuable social networks. These forms of capital can then be converted to economic capital in a cycle of distributional and positional gain. Thus, once socialised into the milieu, golf can provide its members with a great deal of benefits. Stories about these processes in the corporate milieu are lacking at this present time. More qualitative research is required.

REFERENCES

Bourdieu, P. (1986). "The forms of capital". In J. Richardson (Ed.) *Handbook of Theory and Research for the Sociology of Education*, New York, Greenwood, 241-258.

Bourdieu, P. (1999). Scattered Remarks. *European Journal of Social Theory*, 2, 334-340.

Brooke, M. (2015). "Fongzi, dragons and corporate culture: An analysis of corporate dragon-boat paddlers' motivations". *Asia Pacific Journal of Sport and Social Science*, 4*(2)*, 1-12.

Briassoulis, H. (2010). "Sorry golfers, this is not your spot!" Exploring public opposition to golf development. *Journal of Sport and Social Issues*, 34(3), 288-311.

Chew, M. (2013). Why do rich people like to play golf? *Huffington Post.* https://www.huffington post.com/quora/8-reasons-why-the-rich-pl_b_7261994.html

Deal. T.E. and Kennedy, A.A. (1999). *The New Corporate Cultures*. Cambridge: Perseus Publishing.

Donnelly, P. (1996). "The Local and the Global: Globalization in the Sociology of Sport". *Journal of Sport and Social Issues*, 23: 239–57.

Eichberg, H. (2009). "Sport and the Workplace: Company Sport between Corporation and Cooperation". *Sport, Ethics and Philosophy, 3*, 158-170.

Fletcher, R. (2008). "Living on the Edge: The Appeal of Risk Sports for the Professional Middle Class". *Sociology of Sport Journal*, 25*(3)*, 310-330.

Kay, J., & Laberge, S. (2002). "The 'new' corporate habitus in adventure racing". *International Review for the Sociology of Sport*. 37*(1)*, 17–36.

Kuah, K.E. (2007). "Confucian ideology and social engineering in Singapore". *Journal of Contemporary Asia*, 371-383.

Lau, S. (1992). "Collectivism's individualism: Value preference, personal control, and the desire for freedom among Chinese in Mainland China, Hong Kong, and Singapore". *Personality and Individual Differences*. Pp. 361-366.

Lussier, R. N. & Kimball, D. C. (2014). *Applied Sport Management Skills Second Edition with Web Study Guide*. Human Kinetics, US.

Lyng, S. (1990). "Edgework: A social psychological analysis of voluntary risk taking". *American Journal of Sociology*, 95: 851–886.

Peters, T.J. & Waterman, R.H. (1982). *In Search of Excellence*. New York: Warner

Stempel, C. (2005). Adult participation sports as cultural capital: A test of Bourdieu's theory of the field of sports. *International review for the sociology of sport*, 40(4), 411-432.

Thorpe, H. and Wheaton, B. (2011a) "'Generation X Games", action sports and the Olympic movement: Understanding the cultural politics of incorporation', *Sociology,* 45: 830–47.

———. (2011b) 'The Olympic Movement, Action Sports, and the Search for Generation Y', in J. Sugden and A. Tomlinson (Eds), *Watching the Olympics: Politics, Power and Representation*. London: Routledge.

Wilkinson, A. (1998). "Empowerment: theory and practice". *Personnel Review*, 27*(1)*, 40-56.

PART 2:

SOCIALISATION OUT OF SPORT

CHAPTER 5

Muslim Women in Sport

After Ibtihaj Muhammad secured her place in history at the 2016 Rio Olympics, she won a bronze medal for the national US fencing team. However, the focus for her publicity tended to be more connected with her wearing of the hijab during competition. She was the first US athlete to do so and the first hijab-wearing competitor to win a medal. Her victory stirred the long-standing debate about Muslim women's participation in the Olympics. In an interview of August 8th, Ibtihaj Muhammad (https://www.usmagazine.com/celebrity-news/news/ibtihaj-muhammad-first-us-olympian-to-compete-in-hijab-wins-bronze-w434371/) reported:

> 'A lot of people don't believe that Muslim women have voices or that we participate in sport. And it's not just to challenge misconceptions outside the Muslim community, but within the Muslim community. I want to break cultural norms'.

It is a truism that female Muslim athletes remain vastly underrepresented in sport (Walseth, 2006). Sfeir (1985), for example, argues that before 1908, there were no Muslim women in the Olympics. She also states that up until her paper was published in 1984, only 4% of female Olympic participants were Muslim women (p. 287). In 2016, 33 of the 292 female athletes were Muslim women of whom 14 won medals. This shows that there has been an increase in Muslim participation to about 11% from the 4% in 1984. However, this is still a small number. Countries such as Pakistan and Saudi Arabia have very low women participation in sport. Saudi Arabia fielded 4 females in 2016 doubling the 2 at London, 2012.

Sfier (1985) states that the low participation rates are due to institutional constraints on women in these countries. She notes:

> 'There is also the long-standing and persistent obstacle of segregation between the sexes. Most Islamic countries are still unwilling to change the traditional educational system based upon the segregation of sexes. Co-educational institutions and co-educational physical education classes are non-existent and considered irreligious. Another constraint is the lack of sport facilities, particularly of indoor gymnasiums that would allow physical education for girls to be conducted in seclusion' (p. 289).

Women tend to be disciplined by men in some Islamic countries. This seems to be viewed as necessary and a part of the 'symbols of cultural maintenance' (Sfier, 1985, p. 91). The reason for this, often pointed out in research, is that athlete women's identities challenge tradition. These are not viewed as representing a 'respectable femininity' (Walseth, 2006, p. 75). Males, in contrast, are much more readily socialised into sport at all social levels in Islamic countries and thus, more enabled physically. This form of socialisation out of sport is of fundamental concern as it is a human right 'to participate in recreational activities, [and] sports' (United Nations, 1979) and is recognised in the Convention on the Elimination of Discrimination Against Women (CEDAW), and the International Charter of Physical Education and Sport (UNESCO, 1978). Walseth (2006) argues that women in countries like Saudi Arabia often face harassment because of their sport participation. However, as Walseth (2006) points out, there is a tendency to blame Islam for these activities. In fact, it is more closely related to the specifics of certain countries. Ethnicity is not Islam and contrary to widely held beliefs:

> 'Among those [Muslim women] who regard religion (Islam) as a more important source of identification than ethnicity, being physically active is seen as important because of Islam's health aspects' (Walseth, 2006, p. 75).

When women identify more strongly with Islam than their ethnic identity (e.g., Saudi Arabian), exercise is viewed as a very important element of a daily lifestyle. This view is supported by research conducted by Fjogstad (2004), Walseth and Fasting (2003) as well as Abdelrahman (1992). The Prophet Muhammad is said to have stated that: 'The strong believer is better and more beloved to Allah than the weak believer, while there is good in both'. Further, Muhammad appears to have been an active athlete and encouraged parents and children alike to exercise regularly; and his wife, Aisha, also ran and competed against Muhammad. She said, 'I competed with the Messenger of Allah (in running) and overtook him. Later, when I had put on some weight, I once again competed with him, but this time he overtook me and said: 'We're even now' (Qur'an, Hadith 9: 2055, Sunan Ibn Majah cited at https://ummahsports.net/sports-in-islam/). It appears then, in the Qur'an, that there is inclusion in sport for both men and women and even mixed gender competition. Moreover, there is another verse which declares 'be you male or female—you are equal to one another' (Qur'an 3:195, http://www.masjidtucson.org/publications/ books/sp/1998/jun/page1.html). The evidence cited suggests that Islam is non-discriminatory, encouraging gender equality and physical culture alike. Thus, Islam is perhaps not the core reason why Muslim women are socialised out of sport.

However, what is often communicated in the press is that it is the Islamic religion, not the ethnicity, that socialises women out of sport. In an article by Edwards (2016) at The Daily Mail, and this view was also represented in many other media sites at the time of the 2016 Rio Olympics, Ibtihaj Muhammad is described as 'determined to show the world that Muslim-American women can excel in sports' (http://www.dailymail.co.uk/news/article-3739419/Muhammad-US-teammates-win-bronze-sabre-fencing.html). There is a deliberate emphasis on her Muslimness conveying the implicit meaning that it is Islam that restricts women. Further, the hijab is often cited as a hinderance to participation. In March 2007, for example, FIFA banned the hijab in football. Moreover, Ahmad (2011) found that football organisations discriminated against athletes, alienating them for their hijab wearing.

This was described as a 'visible barrier to sport in Britain' (Ahmad, 2011, p. 452). However, in 2014, FIFA lifted the hijab ban stipulating that both men and women can wear head attire if it is the same color as the team's jersey. Nevertheless, despite this, journalists continue to argue that 'hijabs at the Olympics aren't about freedom' (Toronto Sun, 2016 http://torontosun.com/2016/08/10/hijabs-at-olympics-arentaboutfreedom/wcm/82216465-a5f8-410a-9440-782aa1f67f84). It is clear that the niqab and the burka, being full body attire and restricting vision, are strong constraints, socialising women out of sport participation, but the hijab, as a scarf worn on the head to hide the hair, causes no such hindrance for the majority of sports. Indeed, today there are also specialised hijabs for swimming.

The way of perceiving Muslim women as a collective homogeneous concept is an essentialist interpretation of culture. Hamzeh and Oliver (2012) sum this up in their research article:

> 'As such, Muslim students are either a homogeneous group or, in the case of Muslim girls, they are one monolithic group wearing a headscarf' (p. 331).

However, as already noted, Islam is practiced in many countries with very different ethnicities. Thus, to consider Muslims as a homogeneous group, is stereotyping. Sfeir (1985) concludes from her research:

> 'This study also revealed variations in the attitudes of various Islamic societies with regard to the status of women in general and their role in sport. There is no one Islamic society, but a multiplicity of social structures all claiming loyalty to Islam. There is the Arab Islam, Iranian Islam, Turkish Islam, Indonesian Islam etc., which all have different attitudes towards woman's role and status. These different attitudes are related to differences in the complexity of the society and the impact of the whole complex of culture, of economic, religious, political and educational systems' (p. 301).

To support this, in 2014, a survey was conducted from the University of Michigan's Institute for Social Research (as reported by Morin in 2014 at the Pew Research Centre, http://www.pewresearch.org/fact-tank/2014/01/14/qa-with-author-of-u-mich-study-on-preferred-dress-for-women-in-muslim-countries/) on men and women from seven Muslim-majority countries (Egypt, Iraq, Lebanon, Tunisia, Turkey, Pakistan, and Saudi Arabia). Results found that the headscarf was the majority choice in Egypt, Iraq, Tunisia and Turkey; the niqab, or face veil, selected by 63% in Saudi Arabia and 33% in Pakistan; and no head covering in Lebanon was chosen by 50% of those who voted. Men and women shared the same opinions except in Pakistan where men tended to be more conservative.

Therefore, as Bhabha (1994) demonstrates, 'culture' is very complex, and is the product of hegemonic and counter hegemonic processes contesting the social terrain. This also echoes Houlihan's (1994) discussion of the glocal and the creolisation of sport cultures. The local, in this case the different countries stated above, absorbs the global (Islam) and appropriates it to suit its identity. Houlihan (1994) writes that the 'peripheral states are not passive recipients of the imported culture but are in a participative relationship' (p. 365). That is to say, individuals are constrained by, and simultaneously construct, their cultures. Identities are therefore a hybrid of these forces. Hence, research needs to centre on the complex relationships of intersectionality and strive to avoid stereotypification. Hamzeh and Oliver (2012) posit that if this is not done, there is a tendency to produce a racist discourse about Muslim women socialised out of sport because of their religion, even if this does not appear to be the case.

In effect, this ideology can be seen as the 'de-valorizing of non-white cultures' (Razack, 2008, p. 173). Edward Said has written much on Orientalism and its construction. In his 1978 book *Orientalism*, he presents this concept as a means for western cultures to patronise representations of 'The East', such as countries of Asia, North Africa, and the Middle East. Said (1978) argues that the West has been socialised into believing that the Orient is a single social construct and that there is an ontological and epistemological difference between 'the Orient' and 'the Occident'. However, the Orient is only 'an idea' (p. 13). He (1978) furthers that Western scholarship on the East is inextricably linked to imperialism and that the ideology of Orientalism represents attempts to dominate the East. As a collectivisation, and therefore a stereotypification, of many cultures from diverse countries, the term Orientalism sets up opposition between the East and the West and is therefore derisive and used 'as a powerful political instrument of domination' (Said, 1978, pp. 2-3).

The Orient is often perceived as primitive and fanatical. It is regressive and reactionary to the democratic and enlightened ways of the West (Marandi, 2009). Through this form of stereotypification, Orientalism is fictitiously constructed and becomes the non-European Other or 'the strange other' (Ahmed, 2002). The politics of Othering, at the same time, helps the West through a process of self-affirmation and helps to unify its nations and amplify the superiority of its culture. The Orient has helped to construct European culture, and 'helped to define Europe (or the West) as its contrasting image, idea, personality, experience' (Said, 1978, pp. 1-2). This binary relationship produces a limited understanding of the countries in these regions and a view that people are socialised into holding, which is merely a single and limited way of perceiving the world.

Relating this discussion back to Muslim women and sport participation, Islam, as a prevalent religion and way of life in the Orient, is viewed as the cultural source of exclusion and the hijab signals victimhood. However, this understanding of the hijab presented in the West, does not fully seek to uncover the narratives of Muslim women. Hamzeh and Oliver's (2012) work with Muslim girls in the United States concludes that family barriers to sport participation were not constructed based on general principles or religious laws of wearing the hijab. Any socialisation out of sport was based on several discourses regarding identity such as balancing the athletic with the feminine, a common issue amongst all female groups. Consequently, Muslim girls' lives are narratives of negotiations with parents for sport participation, just as in other ethnic communities, including white Caucasian.

To better understand how Muslim culture impacts sport participation, Hamzeh and Oliver (2012) go on to present the hijab as a discourse that extends beyond simply wearing a head scarf. They posit that in the Qur'an, as reported by Mernissi (1995), the hijab also refers to more symbolic spatial and ethical barriers:

> 'The spatial hijab represents the border that restricts female Muslims' mobility in public spaces. The ethical hijab represents the protector that shelters Muslim girls from forbidden things, or harams, such as meeting men alone without the presence of an immediate adult family member, preferably a male' (p. 332).

The term ḥijāb in the Quran is not solely a reference to clothing, but rather a spatial barrier and can be used to concern covering the body, secluding women from public places or in a metaphysical way as 'the veil which separates man or the world from God' (Glasse, 2003, p. 180). The issue is therefore a complex one and it may or may not be caused by religion. An example Hamzeh and Oliver (2012) present from their research is Layla, a 17-year-old, a Muslim Arabian American. Her father prohibits her from swimming as, for him, it violates the ethical hijab, as Layla would be entering the same water as non-Muslims. Three other girls, Dojua, Manal and Abby are also researched in this paper. Both Dojua and Manal could swim with long shorts and long-sleeved shirts while Abby 'had no problem choosing swimming as a physical activity in the study. She was apparently allowed to swim with her two-piece bathing suit anywhere' (Hamzeh & Oliver, 2012, p. 335). The concluding result is that there are 'multiple, fluid interpretations' (Hamzeh & Oliver, 2012, p. 335) of Islam based on how well trust was developed between the girls and their parents. Once the trust was negotiated, these girls were able to make their own choices. Hence, the degree of the hijab interpretation is related to the local; and the ethnicity of the stakeholders.

In countries like Saudi Arabia, Afghanistan and Pakistan, patriarchy is strongly embedded. In Saudi, women need to conform to a set of constraining rules, issued by the Clerics there, regarding sport participation. Human Rights Watch (2012) reports that Saudi Arabia discriminates against women and girls and does not provide them the same opportunities for sport as men and boys (https://www.hrw.org/report/2012/02/15/steps-devil/denial-womens-and-girls-rights-sport-saudi-arabia).
Women are required to train in segregation from men and to perform fully clothed, not only wearing a hijab, but long sleeves and trousers also. At present, until 2018, Saudi women are not even allowed in sport stadiums. When they will be admitted, they will be seated in a segregated area entitled the family zone, away from the men. It is estimated that 90% of women in Pakistan suffer physical abuse; and public floggings of girls and women occur regularly (see for example, the Swat Valley flogging in 2009). It is rather the patriarchal ideology present in these societies, and their interpretations of Islam, that are the causes of these phenomena. Women are not only socialised out of sport in these countries. It is a general law reflected in all public spheres. According to de Knop et al. (1996), patriarchal societies of this nature have striven to construct ideology about purity, such as the hijab on sharing water, in order to isolate and control women (p. 150).

One effective NGO movement that has been developed inside Islamic Afghanistan, to help to empower women there, is Skateistan. Skateboarding plays a unique role in this country where girls are discriminated against at many levels. In this society, when a woman gives birth to a boy, she is welcomed in a ceremony called *Nashrah*, which involves the giving of presents and citation of welcoming prayers (Bezhan & Salih, 2011). If the baby is a girl, on the other hand, 'the woman will be welcomed with mockery, often called a *dokhtar zai*, or *she who only brings daughters* (Sawitri (2017, p.14). Thus, the discrimination starts at birth (Miller, 1984; Pande, 2003). Girls are not considered eligible for sport in Afghanistan. Indeed, bicycle riding is illegal as reported in an ESPN article by Jayme Moye (2014): 'Cultural taboos say it is obscene for a woman to straddle a saddle, and any woman who does is considered amoral'. There have even been instances when girls have been knocked off their bikes, and badly injured, for this act (Moye, 2014). However, as reported in Thorpe & Chawansky (2016), skateboarding was 'brand new' (p. 143) in Afghanistan, and it thus provided 'a loophole' in the patriarchal matrix. As a result, there are many young girls, aged 5–17 who attend the Skateistan programme. Thorpe & Chawansky (2016) interview several members of staff in Kabul and one of them reports that transformations are obvious among their female participants. One member of staff states that the girls 'go from being nervous and giggly and afraid, to being really driven and passionate about a sport, really a go-getter… and it happens faster than I would have ever expected' (p. 144). The centre provides a safe space for these girls to express themselves and be creative through their skating and experience a sense of freedom that is lacking in their social worlds. This kind of movement goes beyond the hijab discourse to look at the real cause of discrimination, patriarchal ideology.

Taks et al. (1994) also bring up the point that little time can be spent on such activities as training for professional sport as a career, without the economic support. Time is a finite resource and using it for sport is a potential loss of earnings. This may impact the number of Muslim women in sport; specifically, it might also be a cause of the low number of Muslim women in sport in more developed countries such as the United Kingdom and North America. Muslims face the greatest hardships of any group in the United Kingdom. According to the 2011 Social Mobility Commission, The Social Mobility Challenges Faced by Young Muslims, only around 20% of the Muslim community is in full-time employment. This is much lower than the average of 33%. Moreover, 46% of the United Kingdom's Muslim population lives in the poorest 10% of inner cities diminishing opportunities for social mobility through education and constraining the number of sports available for development. In these areas, there are few facilities for sport participation. Muslim women are particularly observed to be economically-inactive with 18% reporting that their days are spent 'looking after home and family' (Taks et al. 1994). These challenges must also mean that fewer Muslim women have the opportunity to prepare for a sporting career. This again demonstrates the need to consider intersectionality when analyzing the extent of Muslim women's participation in professional sport.

To sum up, Muslim women's sport participation is connected to a multiplicity of discourses not least of which is patriarchal ideology. The gendering discourse has a profound impact, and, in many cases, it is not the veil that socialises these women out of sport but the interpretation of the hijab as a means for men to dominate women. Further, the low number of Muslim women in professional sport in developed nations could also stem from socio-economic disadvantage. To understand how women from Muslim countries are socialised out of sport, it is important to be aware of the complexity of the issue and not to solely relate it to a head veil. All of the girls on the Skateistan site are wearing clothing covering their bodies as well as their veils under their helmets but this does not appear restrictive for them.

Moreover, contrary to stereotypical Western belief, the hijab is actually viewed by many Muslim women as a positive part of their daily lives. Again, it depends on the degree of interpretation. Many Muslim women choose to wear the hijab as a scarf on their heads. Journalist Imogen Groome (2017) interviewed Nazma Khan, the founder of World Hijab Day. Khan reports how the hijab helps women to dress modestly, a notion that Muslim men also adhere to. She goes on to point out that she has decided to wear the hijab without coercion from her environment and that she is proud to wear it to communicate to the world that she is a Muslim woman who is proactive with her daily religious life. For her, it is an important identifier and enabler. Nazma states:

> 'Every day, hijab gently reminds me to be modest, kind, and honest in my dealings with the world. The hijab also serves as a self-awareness that there's a bigger purpose in life which I need to work toward every day in order to make this world a better place. It's a fulfilling reminder' (http://metro.co.uk/2017/02/21/founder-of-world-hijab-shares-what-wearing-the-hijab-really-means-for-women-6461954/).

This demonstrates that the veil can also carry very positive symbolic meaning for women. It certainly should not prevent them from participating in sport, not even swimming, as noted already.

Today, sporting administrations such as FIFA and the IOC allow veils covering hair to be worn and swimming associations are allowing full body swimwear in competitions. This should therefore not be an issue. The many other discriminatory practices beginning with the value placed on females, and the forms of control relating to patriarchal ideology, as well as socio-economic disadvantage, are what need to be the focus for change. These types of issues act as powerful socializing forces and help to better explain the lack of Muslim women's sport participation.

REFERENCES

Abdelrahman, N.A. (1992). *Women and Sport in the Islamic Society.* Alexandria: Alexandria University.

Ahmed, S. (2002). "This other and other others". *Economy and Society*, 31(4), 558-572.

Ahmad, A. (2011). "British football: where are the Muslim female footballers? Exploring the connections between gender, ethnicity and Islam". *Soccer & Society*, 12(3), 443-456.

al-Qaradawi, Y. (1992). *The lawful and the prohibited in Islam.* Kuwait: International Islamic Federation of Student Organizations.

Bhabha, H. (1994). *The location of culture.* London & New York: Routledge.

Crosby, E. (2014). "Faux Feminism: France's Veil Ban as Orientalism". *Journal of International Women's Studies.* Bridgewater. 15.2: 46-60.

de Knop, P., Theeboom, M., Wittock, H., & de Martelaer, K. (1996). "Implications of Islam on Muslim Girls' Sport Participation in Western Europe. Literature Review and Policy Recommendations for Sport Promotion". *Sport, Education and Society*. Taylor and Francis. 1:2, Pp. 147-164

Edwards, V. (2016). "Muslim fencer who made history as first US Olympian to win medal while wearing a hijab says, 'regardless of faith we can achieve our dreams' in the America that is inclusive". *Daily Mail Online*. Retrieved from http://www.dailymail.co.uk/news/ article-3744520/Muslim-fencer-history-Olympian-win-medal-wearing- hijab-defines-means-American.html

Fjogstad, T. (2004) Muslimske kvinner og fysisk aktivitet og trening i Norge: hvilke muligheter og barrierer står de ovenfor? Oslo: The Norwegian University of Sport and Physical Education.

Glasse, C, (2003). *The New Encyclopedia of Islam*. Rowman Altamira Press.

Hamzeh, M., & Oliver, K. L. (2012). "Because I Am Muslim, I Cannot Wear a Swimsuit Muslim Girls Negotiate Participation Opportunities for Physical Activity". *Research quarterly for exercise and sport*, 83(2), 330-339.

Houlihan, B. (1994) "Homogenization, Americanization and Creolization of Sport: Varieties of Globalisation", *Sociology of Sport Journal*, 11 :356-375.

Howard, G. A. (2016). "Ibtihaj Muhammad Makes History in Rio". *TIME*. Retrieved from http://time.com/4443648/rio-2016-olympics- ibtihaj-muhammad-hijab-history/

Human Rights Watch (2012). "Steps of the Devil." *Denial of Women's and Girls' Rights to Sport in Saudi Arabia* Retrieved from (https://www.hrw.org/report/2012/02/15/steps-devil/denial-womens-and-girls-rights-sport-saudi-arabia).

———— (2016). "Saudi Arabia: Women Are Changing the Game". *Human Rights Watch*. Retrieved from https://www.hrw.org/news/2016/
08/04/saudi-arabia-women-are-changing-game

Malcolm, C. (2016). "Hijabs at Olympics aren't about freedom". *Toronto Sun*. Retrieved from http://www.torontosun.com/2016/08/10/ hijabs-at-olympics-arent-about-freedom

Marandi, S.M. (2009). "Constructing an Axis of Evil: Iranian Memoirs in the Land of the Free". *The American Journal of Islamic Social Sciences: 24*.

Mernissi, F. (1995). *Women and Islam. An Historical and Theological Enquiry*, Oxford: Blackwell Publishers.

Moye, J. (2014). Bravery on a bike in Afghanistan. *ESPN*. Retrieved in November, 2018 from http://www.espn.com/espnw/athletes-life/article/10726599/espnw-afghanistan-women-cycling-team-shows-bravery-resolve.

Nakamura, Y. (2002). "Beyond the hijab: Female Muslims and physical activity". *Women in Sport and Physical Activity Journal*, 11(2), 21-48.

Qur'an. Sahih Hadith 9: 2055, "Sunan Ibn Majah". *Qur'an*. Retrieved from https://sunnah.com/urn/ 1262980

Qur'an. Al-Emran 3:195. *Qur'an*. Retrieved from http://www.comp.leeds.ac.uk/nora/html/3-195.html

Razack, S. (2008). *Casting out: The eviction of Muslims from Western laws & politics*. Toronto, Canada: University of Toronto Press.

Rozenblum, M. (2011). (Director). *Sous La Burqa*. Sasana Productions. Retrieved from http://www.youtube.com/watch?v=jj7cB6DrJ6E

Said, E. (1978). Orientalism. London: Routledge & K. Paul. Pp 7, 12, 172 & 187.

Sawitri, M. Y. (2017). Cultural and International Dissonance on Girls Empowerment: the Case of Afghanistan's Female Son. *Aegis: Journal of International Relations*, 2(1), 11-25

Sfeir, L. (1985). "The status of Muslim women in sport: conflict between cultural tradition and modernization". *International Review for the Sociology of Sport,* 20(4), 283-306.

Stevenson, J., Demack, S., Stiell, B., Abdi, M., Clarkson, L., Ghaffar, F., & Hassan, S. (2017). *The social mobility challenges faced by young Muslims*. Social Mobility Commission. September 2017. Retrieved November, 2018 from http://dera.ioe.ac.uk/29940/1/Young_Muslims_SMC.pdf

Taks, M., Renson, R., & Vanreusel, B. (1994). Of sport, time and money: An economic approach to sport participation. *International Review for the Sociology of Sport, 29*(4), 381-395.

Thorpe, H., & Chawansky, M. (2016). The 'Girl Effect'in action sports for development: The case of the female practitioners of Skateistan. In *Women in Action Sport Cultures* (pp. 133-152). Palgrave Macmillan, London.

Walseth, K. (2006). "Young Muslim women and sport: The impact of identity work". *Leisure studies,* 25(1), 75-94.

Walseth, K. & Fasting, K. (2003) "Islam's view on physical activity and sport Egyptian women interpreting Islam", *International Review for the Sociology of Sport* 38(1), pp. 45–60.

CHAPTER 6

Women in Esports

Esports is an arena that has faced a great deal of criticism over the years. It remains problematic in the field of female participation (Loebenberg, 2018). During an interview with Ong (2017), Peter Souvlis, the director of esports at Australian Esports Media Group, which runs WPGI, the all-girl gaming league in Australia, states that data shows that '52% of video gamers are female' yet the esports world seems to be 'dominated by men' http://www.abc.net.au/news/2017-05-11/women-fighting-pay-disparity-bullying-in-esports/8515202. According to Souvlis, women make up less than 1% of the world's total esports' paid gamers and remuneration considerably differs. The top individual male player earns approximately $2.7 million while the top female players earns around $170, 000. Prize money for men's and women's tournaments is also very different (Loebenberg, 2018). These top players earn from tournaments and are able to stream their skills online to earn a salary, which means that rank and wealth are inextricably linked. A game such as League of Legends (LoL) with a 90% male player-base (Makuch, 2012) has a hierarchy with those who lose games demoted to lower ranks. Additionally, on Twitch, 80% are male players; less than 10% are women (Online Performers Group, 2015). No female gamer has reached the finals in the open tournaments of DOTA 2, League of Legends or Counter-Strike: Global Offensive.

The data above might be used to point to the fact that women are not as talented in the field of esports as men are. This idea has led to the subsequent reasoning behind the all-girls' league and to provide a platform for females to compete and develop their talents. However, this appears illogical in an area of sport where physique should not be as important a variable as it is in traditional sport. Sports such as rugby, in which physical contact is key, might more feasibly argue for gender segregation. So why do female gamers not appear in the open tournaments? It is contended in this chapter that it is not a matter of ability but rather the result of being socialised out of the sporting environment. Hypermasculinity and the resulting gender discrimination act as causes for women's lack of presence in professional esports.

Scharrer (2004) conducted a content analysis of over 1000 advertisements for esports. She found that violence and aggression were very common, and that the representation of women was problematic. She writes:

> 'Female characters appear to be presented with a strong emphasis on body and beauty, often scantily clad and highly sexualized, with exaggerated breast sizes and tiny waists' (p.394).

This also coincides with Beasley and Collins Standley's (2002) study of gender representations in video games. They argue that female characters reveal more skin and a large number (41%) of the characters are 'voluptuous' (p. 394). Similarly, Burgess et al. (2007) conclude that

> 'In spite of their less frequent appearance, female characters were more likely to be portrayed with exaggerated, and often objectified, sexiness. Further, violence and sexiness were paired more frequently for female characters than violence and muscular physiques for the male characters. The potential influence these negative portrayals could have on gamers is discussed' (p. 419).

Thus, representation of women as sexual objects is commonly observed in-game. These are also prevalent outside the virtual environment in cosplay.

The term cosplay (kosupure) is a hybrid of the English 'costume' and 'play'. It was coined by Japanese game creator Tasashi Nobuyuki. For cosplay, people accurately depict the character of a game through appearance and actions. In Japan, women make up the majority of Cosplayers. In 2007, Cure estimated that it was 90% (as cited in Galbraith, 2013). Additionally, cosplay photographers tend to be male and older than their cosplayers (Galbraith, 2013). Women in cosplay out-of-game dress as female in-game characters. Consequently, they tend to also be sexualised. At conventions, women cosplay characters often suffer harassment; so much so that the expression 'creeping at the con' (Bever, 2014) has evolved as a general term. Bever (2014) states that gaming conventions are very much a boy's club and girls need to be careful at conventions.

Doxxing, or finding out a woman's true identity and then stalking her in real life, is not uncommon (Loebenberg, 2018). Trolling with threats of rape and death by male gamers are also common (Shaw, 2015). Anita Sarkeesian, creator of 'Tropes Vs. women in video games' was harassed on and offline. The #GamerGate scandal was an event that led to women game developers being heavily harassed by men on and offline (Chess & Shaw, 2015). Nakandala, Ciampaglia, Su, and Ahn's (2016) study of 76 days of Twitch public chat messages demonstrates that the predominant subjects on channels for women involve terms like 'babe', 'boobs' and 'gorgeous'. League of Legends (LoL), arguably the most popular games, is often host to toxic masculinity (Devia-Allen, 2017). During Capcom's Cross Assault reality show, a competition promoting Street Fighter X Tekken, Aris Bakhtanians, leader of Team Tekken, made derogatory comments about female participants. He further argued that this form of sexual harassment was integral to the gaming culture and its community (Klepek, 2012a, 2012b). Twitch.tv community manager Jared Rea publicly countered this form of harassment and discrimination as it could only further alienate potential female fans from the sport.

A case study reported by Salter and Blodgett (2012), provides further insight into the gendered discourse of esports and the rape culture in gaming. Penny Arcade, a webcomic in gaming culture, was involved in a controversial publication joking about a MMORPG quests whose characters, the Dickwolves, raped their victims. A rape victim spoke against the humour and urged others to boycott Penny Arcade Expo. The Penny Arcade editorship responded by ironically advising those who read the comic to not be influenced into becoming rapists. This demonstrated that the gaming community fostered an aggressive gendered discourse. Subsequently, further rebuke and conflict followed. Nevertheless, Penny Arcade then sold 'Penny Arcade Dickwolves' T-shirts further inciting the community, suggesting that rape survivors should be silenced. In the end, Penny Arcade removed the T-shirts and publicly apologised for these events. However, practices of this nature, that tend to other female participants and boost male domination, cause subjugation of women as they construct barriers that socialise women from the scene. This behaviour cited might be hard-core geek masculinity but toxic trolling in the form of sexist insults appears to be endemic in esports.

Hegemonic masculinity, from Connell (1987), is therefore present in both the in-game and out-of-game cultures of esports. Hegemonic Masculinity extended from Gramsci's Hegemony Theory is a:

> 'Set of values, established by men in power that functions to include and exclude, and to organize society in gender unequal ways. It combines several features: a hierarchy of masculinities, differential access among men to power (over women and other men), and the interplay between men's identity, men's ideals, interactions, power, and patriarchy' (Jewkes and Morrell, 2012, p. 40).

Two forms of Hegemonic Masculinity can be found in esports: external and internal. The first is men over women and the second, men over men. These are defined as the 'institutionalization of men's dominance over women' (Connell, 1987, p. 844) and the 'social ascendancy of one group of men over all other men' (Connell, 1987, p. 844) respectively. The harassment of women appears to be judged as appropriate male domination and is accepted amongst male gamers. It has been termed 'geek masculinity' (Salter & Blodgett, 2012) and is related to the omnipresence of the male gaze (Mulvey, 2009) online. This gaze depicts women from the masculine and heterosexual point of view, comparable to scopophilia, with women as passive and objects of observation. As Tyson (2014) points out, the gaze is when 'the man looks; the woman is looked at. And it is the one looks who is in control, who holds power to name things, the power to explain the world and so to rule the world' (p. 97). Thus, emphasised femininity is very present also. It is a woman's 'compliance to patriarchy' (Schippers, 2007) through the active consent to objectification. In other words, women behave the way that men find them desirable (Taylor, 2012). When women dress as gaming characters in cosplay, they may be viewed as embracing patriarchal ideology and thus, in Gramscian terms, demonstrating 'active consent' to the discrimination. As Theberge and Birrell (1994a) point out 'hegemony is a fairly complete system of ideological dominance that works through the apparent complicity of those disenfranchised by it' (p. 327). Birrell (1998) argues that the body should not be viewed as a site for defining gender relations. Consequently, it is posited that women who look and dress in conformance with the mainstream hetero-male norms of beauty may be doing ill to the feminist cause (Birrell, 1988). Bartky (1988) and Bordo (2003) have emphasised that it produces a Taylorism of the feminine body as a commodity and a femininity of gendered-docility.

This social world of sport, which tends to isolate women, can be viewed using Noelle-Nuemann's (1974) Spiral of Silence (SOS). SOS theory posits that people are less likely to express their views if they perceive these to be the minority opinion. In contrast, the prevalent, majority voice tends to be reiterated and reified consistently. This perpetuates a fear of isolation. This constructs cycles of self-perpetuation and the silence is increasingly accepted as the norm. Lee and Kim (2014) state:

> 'Fear of isolation is a primary concept underlying the psychological mechanism that explains the process of the SOS (Noelle-Neumann, 1974; Scheufele, 2008). Fear of isolation has been used as a main explanation for why a perceived gap with the majority opinion leads to unwillingness to speak out: that is, people who fear being isolated will follow the majority opinion' (Moy et al. 2001; Noelle-Neumann, 1974; Scheufele & Moy, 2000)' (p. 266).

There is clearly evidence that demonstrates women's minority status online, as gaming has always targeted and marketed a male audience.

Because of their minority status and the presence of the SOS, Twitch has established Inclusivity City for diversity organisations (Schmidt, 2016). There are also some advocacy groups working to construct more inclusivity as part of this. AnyKey (https://www.anykey.org/) has been working on the issue of gender discrimination. Its mission is:

> 'To help create fair and inclusive spaces in esports for marginalized members of the gaming community. We pledge to: Provide competitive gamers with resources, support, and opportunities. Highlight positive role-models. Create knowledge and tools to help create more diverse communities and supportive networks' (https://www.anykey.org/about/).

AnyKey concentrates on developing the number of women in eSports. It helps to provide female gamers with financial support and encourage more women into the gaming industry. The two founders are both female. Morgan Romine, Director of Initiatives, was a founder and captain of the Frag Dolls, a female professional gaming team. T.L. Taylor, Director of Research, is a Professor at MIT and author of Raising the Stakes: E-sports and the Professionalisation of Computer Gaming (MIT Press, 2012). Through the organisation of competitions, research and holding workshops, AnyKey seeks to develop awareness of the discrimination facing women in eSports and encouraging more female participation. They provide a platform for public live-streamed panels to share knowledge and discuss potential solutions. This advocacy is clearly required to increase the number of women in eSports (Thursten, 2016). In an interview at a women-only eSports tournament in Katowice, Poland, Romine states:

"There is a lot of work that needs to be done, giving more women confidence and experience in that space" (cited in Schmidt, 2016).

Through this type of sharing, women might be viewed more respectfully by men, and potentially, esports is ideally situated to transcend the patriarchal characteristics of traditional sport. Stereotypical views of women in traditional sport might not spill over to esports as physicality for overcoming an opponent appears to be much less relevant online (Jenny, Manning, Keiper & Olrich, 2016). However, as presented, female gamers rarely appear in teams in open tournaments or in the top echelon of individual games. They are consistently exposed to toxic language on streaming sites such as Twitch. They are also being socialised out of the sporting environment through isolatory tactics from male gamers. The hypermasculinity and the resulting gender discrimination act as causes for women's lack of presence in esports. Notwithstanding, some women persist and speak out about the future of gaming. Stephanie Harvey (missharvey), a well-known professional gamer, believes that is important to dismantle the all-female competitions. She states that companies need to provide more support for women in eSport 'because, in the end, you need money to compete, but ultimately the goal is that these female tournaments do not exist anymore because there's no need for it' (Loop Technology, 2016). Her view is that once women have developed their skills in the all-female competitions, they can shift to the mixed gender gaming scene.

To conclude, female gamers are socialised out of the esports environment. Gender discrimination is practiced through several means and this probably causes women's lack of presence in professional eSport. In-game, characters are often designed to be 'voluptuous' promoting the objectification of women. Toxic language online through media such as Twitch is common also. Out-of-game cosplay as simulation of these characters, often takes on the same emphasised femininity traits leading to actual discrimination at conventions with the phenomenon of 'creeping at the con'. Further, doxxing, a form of stalking a woman in real life, also occurs. These activities lead many critics to conclude that geek masculinity is the cause. It effectively socialises women out of the main prizes and the public eye. Some advocacy bodies are attempting to fight this. Esports is potentially an area where gender is not important. However, at the moment, a great deal of change is required for it to reach the goal of gender equity.

REFERENCES

Admin Dafaesports. (2018). "Intel Extreme Masters". *Dafaesports*. Retrieved from http://en.dafaesports.com/category/tournament/intel-extreme-masters/

Anderson, E. (2008, June). "I used to think women were weak: Orthodox masculinity, gender segregation, and sport". In *Sociological Forum*, 23(2), 257-280. Blackwell Publishing Ltd.

Bartky, S. L. (1988). "Foucault, Femininity, and the Modernization of Patriarchal Power". In R. Weitz (Ed.), *The Politics of Women's Bodies: Sexuality, Appearance, and Behavior*. New York: Oxford University Press.

Beasley, B., & Collins Standley, T. (2002). "Shirts vs. skins: Clothing as indicator of gender role stereotyping in video games". *Mass Communication & Society*, 5, 279–293.

Bever, L (2014). Creeping at a con: sexual harassment at comic-con, not so comic. *Washington Post*. Retrieved November 2018 from https://www.washingtonpost.com/news/morning-

mix/wp/2014/07/28/creeping-at-a-con-sexual-harassment-at-comic-con-not-so-comic/?utm
_term=.535aac412ecc

Birrell, S. J. (1988). "Discourses on the gender/sport relationship: from women in sport to gender relations". *Exercise and sport sciences reviews*, *16*, 459-502.

Bordo, S. (2003). *Unbearable Weight: Feminism, Western Culture, and the Body*. Los Angeles, CA: University of California Press.

Burgess, M. C., Stermer, S. P., & Burgess, S. R. (2007). "Sex, lies, and video games: The portrayal of male and female characters on video game covers". *Sex roles*, *57*(5-6), 419-433.

Chess, S., & Shaw, A. (2015). "A conspiracy of fishes, or, how we learned to stop worrying about# GamerGate and embrace hegemonic masculinity". *Journal of Broadcasting & Electronic Media*, *59*(1), 208-220.

Connell, R. (1987). *Gender and Power: Society, the Person, and Sexual Politics*. Stanford University Press.

Connell, R., & Messerschmidt, J. (2005). "Hegemonic Masculinity: Rethinking the Concept". *Gender and Society*, 19(6), 829-859.

Devia-Allen, G. C. (2017). *Good Game Well Played: An Esports Documentary. Theses and Dissertations*. 663. Illinois State University. Retrieved from http://ir.library.illinoisstate.edu/etd/663

Dill-Shackleford, K. & Thill, K. P. (2007). "Video Game Characters and the Socialization of Gender Roles: Young People's Perceptions Mirror Sexist Media Depictions". *Sex Roles,* 57(11), 851-864.

Fink, J. S. (2015). "Female athletes, women's sport, and the sport media commercial complex: Have we really come a long way, baby?" *Sport Management Review*, 18(3), 331-342.

Galbraith, P. (2013). Cosplay, lolita and gender in Japan and Australia. *Intersections: Gender and Sexuality in the Pacific, 32*. Retrieved Novenber, 2018 from http://intersections.anu.edu.au/issue32/galbraith _intro.htm

Gera, E. (2014). "Where are the women in eSports?" *Polygon*. Retrieved from https://www.polygon.com/2014/5/27/5723446/women-in-esports-professional-gaming-riot-games-blizzard-starcraft-lol

Gramsci, A. (1971). *Selections from the Prison Notebooks of Antonio Gramsci*. Ed. and Transl. by Quintin Hoare and Geoffrey Nowell Smith. New York: International Publishers.

Jenny, S. E., Manning, R. D., Keiper, M. C., & Olrich, T. W. (2017). "Virtual (ly) athletes: Where eSports fit within the definition of sport". *Quest*, *69*(1), 1-18.

Jewkes, R., & Morrell, R. (2012, June). "Sexuality and the limits of agency among South African teenage women: Theorising femininities and their connections to HIV risk practises". *Social Science and Medicine*, 74(11), 1729-1737.

Klepek, P. (2012a). *Aris "Aris" Bakhtanians Releases Statement on Recent Comments*. Retrieved from https://www.giantbomb.com/articles/aris-aris-bakhtanians-releases-statement-on-recent/1100-4007/

———. (2012b). *When Passions Flare, Lines Are Crossed* [UPDATED]. Retrieved from https://www.giantbomb.com/articles/when-passions-flare-lines-are-crossed -updated/1100-4006/.

Lane, S and Jackson, E. (2017). "Female gamers face sexism and bullying in e-sports competitions", *ABC*. Retrieved from http://www.abc.net.au/radio/programs/am/female-gamers-face-sexism-and-bullying-in-e-sports/8516486

Lee, N. Y., & Kim, Y. (2014). "The spiral of silence and journalists' outspokenness on Twitter". *Asian Journal of Communication*, *24*(3), 262-278.

Loebenberg, A. (2018). "What is the state of play?" *International Journal of Play*, 1-5.

Loop Technology (2016). *The women challenging sexism in esport*. http://www.looppng.com/content/women-challenging-sexism-e-sports

Makuch, E. (2012). *Riot: League of Legends has 12 million daily 'active' players*. Gamespot.com. Retrieved from https://www.gamespot.com/articles/riot-league-of-legends-has-12-million-daily-active-players/1100-6398154/

Martončik, M. (2015). "e-Sports: Playing just for fun or playing to satisfy life goals?" *Computers in Human Behavior, 48*, 208-211.

Mulvey, L. (2009). "Visual pleasure and narrative cinema" in Laura Mulvey, Laura, *Visual and other pleasures* (2nd ed.), Houndmills, Basingstoke, Hampshire England, New York: Palgrave Macmillan, pp. 14–30.

Nakandala, S., Ciampaglia, G., Su, N.M., & Ahn, Y.-Y. (2016). *Gendered conversation in a social game-streaming platform*. Retrieved from https://arxiv.org/pdf/1611.06459.pdf

Newman, J. A. & White, L.A. (2012). *Women, Politics, and Public Policy: The Political Struggles of Canadian Women* (2nd Ed.). Toronto: Oxford University Press.

Ong, T. (2017). *The female gamers fighting bullying in eSports. ABC News Australia*. Retrieved from http://www.abc.net.au/news/2017-05-11/women-fighting-pay-disparity-bullying-in-esports/8515202.

Online Performers Group. (2015). *Twitch gender study infogram, charts & infographics*. Retrieved from https://infogr.am/twitch_gender_study

Saedler, P. (2017). "Team Secret win it all at Intel Challenge Katowice 2017". *ESL*. Retrieved from https://www.eslgaming.com/article/team-secret-win-it-all-intel-challenge-katowice-2017-3441.

Salter, A., & Blodgett, B. (2012). "Hypermasculinity & dickwolves: The contentious role of women in the new gaming public". *Journal of broadcasting & electronic media, 56*(3), 401-416.

Scharrer, E. (2004). "Virtual violence: Gender and aggression in video game advertisements". *Mass Communication & Society*, 7(4), 393-412.

Schippers, M. (2007). Recovering the feminine other: Masculinity, femininity, and gender hegemony. *Theory and society, 36*(1), 85-102.

Schmidt, G. (December 21, 2016). Esports sees profit in attracting female gamers. (Online), April 11, 2017. The New York Times. https://www.nytimes.com/2016/12/21/technology/personaltech/video-game-makers-try-to-get-better-at-luring-women-to-esports.html *(PDF) Gender Inequality in eSports Participation: Examining League of Legends*. Available from:https://www.researchgate.net/publication/326560970_Gender_Inequality_in_eSports_Participation_Examining_League_of_Legends [accessed Dec 23 2018].

Shaw, A. (2015). *Gaming at the edge: Sexuality and gender at the margins of gamer culture*. Minneapolis: University of Minnesota Press.

Taylor, T. L. (2012). *Raising the Stakes: E-sports and the Professionalization of Computer Gaming*. Mit Press.

Theberge, N., & Birrell, S. (1994). "The sociological study of women and sport". *Women and sport: Interdisciplinary perspectives*, 323-330.

Thursten, C. (2016). *AnyKey on a year spent advancing the cause of diversity in esports*. Retrieved from http://www.pcgamer.com/anykey-on-a-year-spent-advancing-the-cause-of-diversity-in-esports/

Tyson, L. (2014). *Critical theory today: A user-friendly guide*. Routledge.

Wagner, M. G. (2006, June). "On the Scientific Relevance of eSports". In proceedings of *International Conference on Internet Computing* (pp. 437-442).

Yao, M. Z., Mahood, C., & Linz, D. (2010). "Sexual Priming, Gender Stereotyping, and Likelihood to Sexually Harass: Examining the Cognitive Effects of Playing a Sexually-Explicit Video Game". *Sex Roles, 62*(1-2), 77–88.

CHAPTER 7

The Case of Intersex Athletes

Holmes (2002) states that:

> 'Intersexuality is a historical and cultural construction rather than a simple biological phenomenon. The categorization of intersex is related to ideological commitments to a presumed binary "nature" of male and female, coupled with a paradoxical assumption that gender is so fluid that we are entitled to make of infants and children whatever we will' (p. 175).

This issue of intersex athletes is extremely problematic in elite sport as it is a sex-segregated milieu and one that is, and remains to be, constructed on patriarchal principles and myths about sport and fairness as well as national identity and femininity. In this way, intersex athletes are socialised out of sport.

The way the International Association of Athletics Federation (IAAF) has treated these athletes is inconsistent and at times, illogical. Having won the African 800m race in the 2009 World Track and Field Championships title, Caster Semenya, was required to do a sex-verification test. She was subsequently banned for 11 months from competing due to the unfair advantage that her intersex identity gave her. In Rio 2016, she competed again and won the gold medal in the 800-meter event. After the race, the 6th place Lynsey Sharp, displayed her anxiety; crying, she said 'everyone can see it's two separate races so there's nothing I can do' (https://www.independent.co.uk/sport/olympics/rio-2016-caster-semenyas-800m-win-lynsey-sharp-tears-intersex-debate-a7202251.html).

In 2014, after winning the Asian Junior Athletics Championships 200-meter sprint and 4-by-400- relay in Taipei, Taiwan, Dutee Chand was asked by the Athletics Federation of India, regional body of the International Association of Athletics Federations (I.A.A.F.), to go to Delhi for routine urine and blood tests. However, on arrival, she underwent ultrasound instead. A few days later, the Indian government's sport authority followed up with a letter stating:

> 'It has been brought to the notice of the undersigned that there are definite doubts regarding the gender of an Athlete Ms. Dutee Chand' (reported in the New York Times Magazine http://www.queercsuf.com/wgst100/wgst100_readings/humiliating_practice_sex_testingfemale_athletesnyt.pdf).

In the *New York Times Magazine* (https://www.nytimes.com/2016/07/03/magazine/the-humiliating-practice-of-sex-testing-female-athletes.html), Padawer (2016) points out that there are many conditions that might appear to be characteristics of intersex people. Some experts predict that it might include 1 in 60 people. Trying to explain the physiological debate, she writes:

'Some intersex women, for instance, have XX chromosomes and ovaries, but because of a genetic quirk are born with ambiguous genitalia, neither male nor female. Others have XY chromosomes and undescended testes, but a mutation affecting a key enzyme makes them appear female at birth; they're raised as girls, though at puberty, rising testosterone levels spur a deeper voice, an elongated clitoris and increased muscle mass. Still other intersex women have XY chromosomes and internal testes but appear female their whole lives, developing rounded hips and breasts, because their cells are insensitive to testosterone. They, like others, may never know their sex development was unusual, unless they're tested for infertility or to compete in world-class sports' (p. 3).

The female range of testosterone is between 1.0 to 3.3 nanomoles per litre of blood, which is about 10% that of males. Chand's level entered the 'male range rising above the 10-nanomoles-per-liter limit the I.A.A.F uses for female athletes. Tracey Lambrechs, a New Zealand weightlifter changed to a different weight category to avoid competing against a male to female athlete Laurel Hubbard. She declared: "I feel there is an unfair advantage even though it is within the regulations. All I can hope is that they look into it and make a more educated judgment" (http://www.breitbart.com/sports/2017/11/27/biological-male-weightlifting-champ-qualifies-womens-competition-new-zealand/).

This is not a new phenomenon. Renee Richard was not allowed to compete in the 1976 US Open due to her male-to-female sex reassignment surgery. She fought the decision and, in 1977, the New York Supreme Court agreed that it was a case of sex discrimination. As early as the 1936 Olympics when American Helen Stephens, the Missouri Express, won the 100-metre race setting a new world record. Outcry at the performance led to queries over her gender. Skepticism of this kind towards female athletes continued throughout the cold war, particularly as the Soviet Union picked up the majority of the women's medals in gymnastics and athletics. In 1952, the Soviets won 11 from 21 medals in women's gymnastics and 11 from 27 in women's athletics at the Helsinki Olympics. The *Washington Post* journalist, Shirley Povich, interpreted the Soviet women's successes in Finland as a negative reflection of their physicality:

'These 1952 Games wouldn't even have been close between Russia and the USA save for the almost complete dominance of the Russian women in the heftier field events and the gymnastics. In the non-bicep division, though, in the more graceful swimming and diving events where feminine form counts more than feminine muscle, the American girls were all-conquering. Each to her liking, perhaps' (cited in Pieper, 2014, p. 1561).

Clearly those women are masculinised and discriminated against for this. According to Cahn (1994), they were Othered as 'Amazons from the Russian steppes' and in this way, the Americans could make up for their lack of achievements. Indeed, Collins (2004) argues that the way the African American woman athlete is portrayed today is similar to the Soviet Othering practices during the Cold War.

Despite calls for better treatment of intersex athletes, gender discrimination in many forms continues leading to socialisation out of sport. The cases above demonstrate how the gender binary is still prevalent in sport and how it uses the 'fair play' and 'unfair advantage' narratives. It also forces transgender athletes to conform to one or the other binary genders. Athletes who do not are depicted as abnormal. However, as Foddy and Savulescu (2011) argue, 'gender is not a binary quantity' (p. 1184) and any form of segregation based on gender should be considered as an 'inconsistent and unjust policy' (Foddy & Savulescu, 2011, p. 1184). Gender is a very complex fluid notion but chances to maintain this perspective were destroyed, as Reis (2009) demonstrates, during the 18th and 19th centuries. During this period, even though there were many cultures that condoned a range of sexualities, including native American, European colonisers and Western medical practitioners secured the binary generalisation. This was based on a vision of the Western, often Christian image, of the feminine lady and masculine man.

By critiquing women in this way about their sex identification, women are measured compared to men. According to MacKinnon's (1987) Dominance Feminist Theory:

> 'Under the sameness standard, women are measured according to our correspondence with men, our equality judged by our proximity to his measure. Under the difference standard, we are measured according to lack of correspondence with him, our womanhood judged by our distance from his measure' (p.34).

Treatment of transgendered individuals helps to confirm and promote hegemonic masculinity, practices that subordinate women. This also discriminates against men who do not fit into the hypermasculine prototype (Connell, 1987). As Sullivan (2011) points out, the fairness debate about transgender athletes, such as Semenya, represents ideology constraining the female body's performance and structuring its form.

Gender testing only involves athletes who transit from male to female to test for female hyperandrogenism and this sends the message that the male is the dominant sex. The underlying argument is that transiting from male to female gives an athlete advantage, but it is not the case for female to male. Additionally, it is assumed that a higher testosterone level provides a better sporting performance. A common concern for unfair advantage theorists is that male to female athletes might benefit from biological superiority in features such as muscle mass or lung capacity (see Papadimitriou et al. 2016). Gooren and Bunck (2004) concluded that muscle mass was much higher in transgender females who had not received hormone replacement therapy (HRT). However, this is repudiated in other research. In the journal *Scientific American,* it is concluded that there is no scientific evidence to prove that this is the case. The editors state: 'it is unscientific and unfair to bar female athletes with elevated testosterone' (https://www.scientificamerican.com/article/naturally-

occurring-high-testosterone-shouldn-t-keep-female-athletes-out-of-competition/).
Moreover, Dr. Eric Vilain, medical geneticist, involved in the IOC's testosterone level policy, has conceded that it 'is not and cannot be perfect' to determine if advantage can be wrought from one factor alone (as reported in Howell, 2013). Hence, this is not a fair reason to socialise transgendered athletes out of sport.

Furthermore, physical equality, no matter how much a focus, is never attained. Coggon, Hammond & Holm (2008) point out that the natural lottery is not considered unfair or at least, it is tolerated. Finnish skier Eero Mäntyranta's had a genetic mutation providing him with a 65% red blood cell count higher than the average male. He was unstoppable during his career. Swimmers such as Thorpe and Phelps had optimum wing spans and feet size to provide them with advantages over their opponents. These physical inequalities match the benefits an athlete may reap from hyperandrogenism but are not considered in the advantage debate in elite competition. As Sullivan (2011) states:

> 'Within the "advantage thesis" discourse, assumptions of fairness appear to receive priority over the impact of discrimination. Other types of classifications systems that fit within the fair play discourse have rarely been addressed' (p. 415).

Sullivan (2011) goes on to point out that hormone levels, to identify athletes with hyperandrogenism, are tested for in the same way as performance enhancing drugs; with one distinction, which is that the former is a natural phenomenon; the latter, a form of cheating. Being discriminated against for one's sexuality, and made to feel abnormal, is the impact of this system.

It seems therefore that what is being questioned is not natural advantage but gender. According to bioethicist Katrina Karkazis, as reported in a New York Times article (https://www.nytimes.com/2016/08/20/sports/caster-semenya-800-meters.html), the opposition to athletes like Semenya is fear of a 'gender apocalypse'; that the binary will be dropped and that women can compete with men on a par. However, this fear has always existed in elite sport and women have suffered exclusion from sport historically due to this (Rowe, 2016). De Coubertin (1912) exclaimed that the purpose of the Olympics was:

> 'The solemn and periodic exaltation of male athleticism, based on internationalism, by means of fairness, in an athletic setting, with the applause of women as the reward' (1912b, lines 54-56).

Gender-segregation and gender testing is evidence of this continued male superiority.

The history of gender testing demonstrates that this form of socialisation out of sport is both humiliating and ineffective. In the past, non-cisgender individuals were required to demonstrate that their sex was the same as that at birth through a mandatory check on their external genitalia conducted by gynecologists during what was termed 'naked parades' (see Sullivan, 2011). The IOC realised that this test was humiliating and degrading and sought less intrusive measures. In 1968, a new test based on chromosomal markers was introduced in its place through buccal smear. All women underwent the test and having successfully met requirements, they were administered a 'fem card' or certification of gender which they were asked to carry with them (Sullivan, 2011). However, as already stated, Padawer (2016) clearly argues that there is no full-proof testing for gender in this way and there have been several incidents proving this. Polish sprinter Ewa Klobukowska failed the test and was stripped of her Olympic medals and the 100-meter world record effaced, and she was not allowed to further compete in any Olympic competitions. She went on to mother a child (Sullivan, 2011, p. 405). In 1985, Maria Jose Martinez Patino failed the gender test and was ousted from competition. She said of the ordeal:

> 'What happened to me was like being raped. It must be the same sense of violation and shame. Only in my case, the whole world watched…' (cited in Sullivan, 2011, p. 405).

It was later discovered that she had androgen insensitivity syndrome (AIS), a condition with which a person has male and female traits. Patino fought her disqualification through a legal campaign and requalified as a woman able to compete again in 1988 (Sullivan, 2011, p. 406). In 1996, eight women were tested positive and were found to have AIS also. They were at first disqualified but then reinstated and allowed to compete at the Olympics in Atlanta in 1996. In 1999, the IOC dropped these testing practices but in suspicious cases, reserved the right to conduct them (Sullivan, 2011). However, due to the case of Semenya, gender verification for the 2012, London Olympics was reconducted. In 2017, testing was again dropped as Hyperandrogenism is recognised officially now by the IAAF as not as important as previously viewed. The Court of Arbitration for Sport has suspended the testosterone testing policy to determine whether fairness is violated as it is unable to be sure that 'hyperandrogenic female athletes may benefit from such a significant performance advantage that it is necessary to exclude them from competing in the female category' (as reported by Longman, 2016, in the *New York Times*). This suspension, against whom the IOC has referred as 'deviant' women (Karkazis et al. 2012) can only be welcome as this kind of policing and socialisation out of sport goes against basic human rights.

Cavanagh and Sykes (2006) explain how:

> 'Transsexuals and intersexed athletes—the groups most often subject to discrimination and disqualification—have always confounded a static and unchanging two sex models based on biology, and so their gendered subjectivities were erased (Namaste, 2000) and/or largely ignored in competitive sport prior to the 21st century' (p. 77).

Diverse markers have been used to attempt to define gender and force the male-female binary prototype. However, as the history of testing tells us, such a divide does not exist. Additionally, the 'advantage thesis' appears to be based more on a patriarchal myth than reality. Laurel Hubbard was selected to compete for New

Zealand in the 2018 Commonwealth Games. Taine Polkinghorne, human rights advisor for sexual orientation, gender identity, and sex characteristics (SOGISC), has made it very clear that this selection is only a result of performance and no other factor should be considered (as cited in Caldwell, 2017). Additionally, as we move forward to the Tokyo Games in 2020, mixed-gender events in athletics, swimming, table tennis and triathlon will be taking place. This decision could help to transcend this issue and enable athletes to compete within the category that they feel most comfortable. It is that which surely must be the ideal of inclusivity in sport.

REFERENCES

Cahn, S. K. (1994). *Coming on Strong: Gender and Sexuality in Twentieth-Century Women's Sport.* Cambridge, MA: Harvard University Press.

Caldwell, O. (2017), *Stuff.* Retrieved from https://www.stuff.co.nz/sport/other-sports/99294375/human-rights-commission-nz-backs-transgender-weightlifter-laurel-hubbard-for-commonwealth-games

Cavanagh, S. L., & Sykes, H. (2006). "Transsexual bodies at the Olympics: The International Olympic Committee's policy on transsexual athletes at the 2004 Athens summer games". *Body & Society,* 12(3), 75-102.

Coggon, J., Hammond, N., & Holm, S. R. (2008). "Transsexuals in sport–fairness and freedom, regulation and law". *Sports Ethics and Philosophy,* 2(1), 4-17.

Collins, P. H. (2004). *Black Sexual Politics: African Americans, Gender, and the New Racism.* New York: Routledge.

Connell, B. (2002). "Hegemonic Masculinity". In S. Jackson & S. Scott (Eds). Gender: A *Sociological Reader.* Psychology Press. Pp. 60-63.

De Coubertin, P. (1912). "The Women at the Olympic Games". Cited in Scambler, G. (2005). *Sport and society: history, power and culture.* McGraw-Hill Education (UK). P. 172.

Foddy, B., & Savulescu, J. (2011). "Time to re-evaluate gender segregation in athletics?" *Br J Sports Med,* 45(15), 1184-1188.

Gooren, L. J., & Bunck, M. C. (2004). *Androgen replacement therapy.* Drugs, 64(17), 1861-1891.

Holmes, M. (2002). "Rethinking the meaning and management of intersexuality". *Sexualities,* 5(2), 159-180.

Howell, J. B. (2013). *From Monsters to "Women": Science, Sex, Sport, and the Story of Caster Semenya* (Doctoral dissertation, University of Kansas).

Kane, M. J. (1995). "Resistance/transformation of the oppositional binary: Exposing sport as a continuum". *Journal of Sport and Social Issues,* 19(2), 191-218.

Karkazis, K., Jordan-Young, R., Davis, G., & Camporesi, S. (2012). Out of bounds? A critique of the new policies on hyperandrogenism in elite female athletes. *The American Journal of Bioethics, 12*(7), 3-16.

Kelner, M. (2017). "Caster Semenya storms to third world 800m gold to leave trouble behind". *The Guardian.* London. Retrieved from https://www.theguardian.com/sport/2017/aug/13/caster-semenya-800m-gold-london

Longman, J. (2016). "Understanding the Controversy Over Caster Semenya". *The New York Times.* Retrieved from https://www.nytimes.com/2016/08/20/sports/caster-semenya-800-meters.html.

MacKinnon, C. A. (1987). *Difference and Dominance: On Sex Discrimination.* Cambridge, MA: Harvard University Press. USA.

Padawer, R. (2016). "The Humiliating Practice of Sex-Testing Female Athletes". *New York Times Magazine.* Retrieved from https://www.nytimes.com/2016/07/03/magazine/the-humiliating-practice-of-sex-testing-female-athletes.html

Papadimitriou, I. D., Lucia, A., Pitsiladis, Y. P., Pushkarev, V. P., Dyatlov, D. A., Orekhov, E. F., & Cieszczyk, P. (2016). "ACTN3 R577X and ACE I/D gene variants influence performance in elite sprinters: a multi-cohort study". *BMC genomics*, 17(1), 285.

Pieper, L. P. (2014). "Sex testing and the maintenance of western femininity in international sport". *The International Journal of the History of Sport*, 31(13), 1557-1576.

Reis, E. (2009). *Bodies in Doubt: An American History of Intersex*. Baltimore, MD: John Hopkins University Press. USA.

Rowe, D. (2016). *Sports, Sexism and the Law: Some Contextual History*. The Western Sydney University Press. Australia.

Scientific American (2016). *Naturally Occurring High Testosterone Shouldn't Keep Female Athletes out of Competition*. Retrieved from https://www.scientificamerican.com/article/naturally-occurring-high-testosterone-shouldn-t-keep-female-athletes-out-of-competition/

Sullivan, C. F. (2011). "Gender VErification and Gender Policies in Elite Sport: Eligibility and Fair Play". *Journal of Sport and Social Issues*, 35, (4), 400-419.

WND. (2017). *Female athletes crushed by 'women who were once men'*. Retrieved from: http://www.wnd.com/2017/03/female-athletes-crushed-by-women-who-were-once-men/

PART 3:

SOCIALISATION THROUGH SPORT

CHAPTER 8

(Dis)empowerment for Para-Olympians

In the introduction, it was noted that for Mead (1934), identity is a construct of social interaction, not a biological concept. Identity emerges through socialisation processes. This chapter explores how the identities of people with physical disabilities are constructed through the Paralympic movement. The meaning of Olympism is to 'create a way of life based on respect for universal fundamental ethical principles' (https://www.olympic.org/the-ioc/promote-olympism) and to 'promote a peaceful society concerned with the preservation of human dignity' with a view to positioning 'sport at the service of the harmonious development of humankind'. Similarly, the International Paralympic Committee's vision is to 'enable Paralympic athletes to achieve sporting excellence and inspire and excite the world' to make a 'better world for all people with a disability' (https://www.paralympic.org/the-ipc/about-us).

The Olympic or Paralympic Games are viewed as platforms for communicating human rights development and particularly a decrease in exclusionary practices. They can therefore be viewed as powerful socialising mechanisms. Host nations of the games are commonly observed reinforcing this. Nicholas Cull of the University of Southern Carolina was an informal policy advisor to the House of Commons Foreign Affairs Select Committee on Foreign and Commonwealth Office Public Diplomacy in the UK before London 2012. He referred to the potential of the Paralympic Games:

> 'There are many countries around the world in which differently-abled people do not have the opportunities they enjoy in Britain, and by increasing international exposure to the Paralympics emphasis on what people can do the FCO is performing a significant act of ethical leadership and associating the UK with some truly inspirational people' (as cited in Beacom & Brittain, 2016, p. 276).

Further, at the same time, Conrad Bird, from Public Diplomacy at the Foreign and Commonwealth Office boasted that Britain was an inclusive society. There was also an appointment of Paralympic gold medalist, Tanni-Grey Thompson, as Olympic ambassador. Bird stated: "We felt that the Paralympics was a good opportunity to demonstrate British attitudes toward disability" (cited in Beacom, 2018, p. 356). As a result, it is evident that human rights are linked to the discourse of the Paralympic Games. It is hoped that people are socialised through sport to view the disabled in a positive way.

However, as Beacom and Brittain (2016) point out, in resource-poor regions and those nations who do not openly tolerate and support equality for people with physical disabilities, this might not yet be the case (p. 275). Beacom and Brittain (2016) argue that the Paralympics are therefore subject to limitations in disability advocacy, with only 20% of nations in the Olympics fielding Paralympic athletes (Beacom & Brittain, 2016). Those nations who do not field para-athletes are increasingly viewed as uncommitted to the disability rights advocacy movement and cold to its diplomatic potential for empowerment. These uncommitted nations do not facilitate the empowerment of the processes of socialisation through sport.

In post-WWII England, sport for the impaired developed strongly. Its origin was as rehabilitation of disabled war combatants. Dr. Ludwig Guttmann initiated a spinal injuries centre at the Stoke Mandeville Hospital in Great Britain. From that moment, wheelchair athletes were socialised into taking part in the Stoke Mandeville Games every year for empowerment, but in 1952, Dutch veterans also participated. Guttmann then renamed the event the International Stoke Mandeville Games. In 1959, the International Stoke Mandeville Games Committee, responsible for the organisation of the Games was founded and in 1972 was renamed the International Stoke Mandeville Games Federation (ISMGF). In 1990, the ISMGF transformed to the International Stoke Mandeville Wheelchair Sports Federation (ISMWSF) and was a major actor in the development of the Paralympic Games. In other regions, and from around 1960 also, the World Veterans' Federation met and in 1961 an International Working Group on Sport for the Disabled was constructed to explore how sport could benefit all the disabled, not only the wheelchair-bound.

In 1964, the International Sports Organisation for the Disabled was established. ISOD extended its parameters to include the visually impaired, amputees and cerebral palsy sufferers. In Toronto 1976, the first athlete with a visual impairment participated in the Paralympic Games and in Arnhem in 1980, the first cerebral palsy athlete competed. Since then, three other disability groups have joined the IPC. It is now made up of the CPISRA (Cerebral Palsy International Sport and Recreation Association); IBSA (International Blind Sports Federation); INAS-FID (International Sports Federation for Persons with Intellectual Disability) and IWAS (International Wheelchair and Amputee Sports Federation and CISS, The International Committee of Sport for the Deaf. From 1982, these 4 groups merged and became the 'International Co-ordinating Committee (ICC) of World Sports Organisations for the Disabled'. Then, in 1989, the International Paralympic Committee (IPC) was founded from this merger in Dusseldorf, Germany.

The forming of the International Paralympic Movement in 1989 as a global unified body demonstrated a strong commitment for public diplomacy and empowerment for the physically disabled community. Today it might be seen as a force for socialisation through sport as an 'advocacy body engaged through public diplomacy in promoting disability rights' (Beacom & Brittain, 2016 p. 273). Since this time, the Paralympic movement has increasingly shifted from sport as rehabilitation to sport as competitive elite para-sport. For public diplomacy, the message is that the disabled community is not a deficient or needy one. The public is socialised into receiving this message through sport. The IPC's vision as an advocacy body committed to elite sport for the disabled is clearly enunciated in its 2013 Brand Book (http://www.snpc.org.sg/paralympic-movement/):

'The Paralympic Movement is athlete-focused. Through athletes' stories and achievements, attitudes towards people with an impairment can be changed. They engage and motivate people to create a more inclusive society. The Paralympic Movement builds a bridge which links sport with social awareness to help forge a path for this change and spread the message of respect and equal opportunity for all individuals'.

Elite para-athletes can demonstrate that people with disabilities are not deficient. Hence, the identity of people with disabilities can be positively impacted through sport. This message can increase the movement and move towards a more inclusive environment.

Since its inception in 1960, in Italy when 328 athletes from 21 countries, the Para Games have grown substantially. In 2012, 4,237 athletes from 164 countries were involved in 20 sports. In 2016, the IPC announced that over 2 million tickets had been sold for the Rio games and these games reached a cumulative TV audience of more than 4.1 billion people in more than 150 countries. This represented a growth of 127% in TV viewership compared to the Games in Greece in 2004. This extensive development has conveyed the message that the para-sporting experience can provide competition as worthy as its parallel Games. According to Beacom and Brittain (2016), in the post 9/11 world, the IPC has become 'inherently diplomatic, challenging the world view on disability' (p. 278). One of the most fundamental reasons for developing the movement further is to 'engender public empathy' towards physical disability through sport (p. 279). Beacom and Brittain (2016) even go so far as to say that through their regional IPC associations, 'states vie with one another to enhance their reputation regarding civil liberty and inclusion' (p. 278). Additionally, as Beacom and Brittain (2016) state, the Para Games helps to offer a forum to develop the 'profile of senior politicians domestically and internationally' (p. 280).

From the above, it is clear that the role of the IPC and the games is a fundamental one and that the intended consequences of the movement to help socialise the physically disabled through sport into a more positive and prominent status in society. The movement seeks to demonstrate that this community is not needy and encourages nations across the globe to be involved in this empowerment. Moreover, on a more micro level, several studies demonstrate that a person with a physical disability can find enjoyment through sport (Brittain, 2004; Yeam & Brooke, 2016) and that this might be directly related to self-esteem development (Brittain, 2004). Wolbring (2012) expostulates:

'how disabled people perceive their bodies and their functions, their social reality, affects what they will do to their body, which in turn influences their self-perception, their self-identity and their goals' (p. 254).

Lundberg, Bennett & Smith (2011) present the benefit of adaptive sports in the development of the quality of life of people with physical disabilities. This participation can not only lead to positive psycho-social effects, but also challenge stereotypes. These are also said to be positive impacts of sport socialisation.

Further, the abilities of the para-athletes and their use of technology such as the prosthetic (in Greek meaning 'an addition to remove physical stigma') has transformed and empowered the physically-impaired body. Prosthesis innovations have grown to be a very important element of the games today resulting in empowerment (Gethins, 2014). A former professional Paralympian athlete and advocate of prosthetic aesthetics is Aimee Mullins who became the first user of the 'Cheetah' woven-carbon-fiber prosthetic sprinting blades in the 1996 Atlanta Para-games. She now promotes this body aesthetics technology as a fashion model and has been known to wear skillfully hand-carved wooden prosthetic legs (Persson, 2017). She also wears prostheses with smart skin, making it very possible to resemble a human leg. From this view, prostheses are not just covering but creating a positive image to challenge stigma. Mullins was the United States' Chef de Mission during the 2012 Summer Olympics and Paralympics. Additionally, the success of athlete Oscar Pistorius, the 'fastest man on no legs', a bilateral-below-the-knee amputee, demonstrated that para-athletes can compete with Olympic athletes. He competed with carbon-fibre blades, in the London 2012 400-meter semi-final competition against able-bodied athletes. During the race, 80,000 people applauded him (Donnelly, 2012). At the end of this race, champion Grenada's Kirani James exchanged his race tag with Pistorius and in an interview stated: "He is out here making history and we should all respect that and admire that" (Donnelly, 2012).

Athletes of this caliber help humanity to look forward to a new era in which technology is inextricably linked to what it means to be human. Those who seek to thwart progress are criticised as conformists to Status Quo Bias (Bostrom & Ord, 2006). This is the future as envisaged by Transhumanists. Nick Bostrom (2005) defines transhumanism as one which 'promotes an interdisciplinary approach to understanding and evaluating the opportunities for enhancing the human condition and the human organism opened up by the advancement of technology' (p.1). Human nature is a 'work-in-progress, a half-baked beginning that we can learn to remould in desirable ways' (Bostrom, 2003, p. 493). Technological progress then can be partly viewed as the deliberate construction of instrumentally-useful tools to alleviate our biological shortcomings. The impaired are technically-enabled through their sport participation.

At the same time however, as technology has progressed, and the use of enhancements has increasingly become a part of the sport vernacular, there has been a concern that a new inequality is emerging. This form of socialisation through sport might be more controversial. As Wolbring (2012) notes, it is no longer a question of mimicking expected body functioning but perhaps the 'prospect of people labelled as impaired outperforming the so called non-impaired person in general and the Paralympic athlete outperforming Olympic athletes' (p. 251). In consequence, the technology-enhanced Paralympic movement could help humanity to transcend its species-typical boundaries (Bostrom 2003; Roco & Bainsbridge 2003; Wolbring 2008a; 2008b; 2008c). This raises concerns about the movement and terms negatively labelling the 'cheetah' woven-carbon-fiber prosthetic sprinting blades as 'techno doping devices' have emerged. In this respect, the physically disabled might be empowered through technology to surpass their able-bodied counterparts. This new inequality is a potentially significant form of socialisation through sport and potential development of positive identity construction for the disabled community.

Further, despite the evident role that the Paralympics may play as a useful platform for empowerment, there are also unintended consequences of the event that contradict this as idealism. Aiden and McCarthy (2014) report the post-London Games of 2012:

> 'Half (58%) of disabled people responding to a survey in 2013 said that they had not noticed any change in people's attitudes towards them as a disabled person following the 2012 Paralympic Games a major moment for disability in the UK. [12] One in five (22%) were of the opinion that people's attitudes have worsened, while less than one in ten (9%) believed people's attitudes towards disabled people have improved' (p. 9).

With this in mind, what might be the causes of the 22% decline in people's attitudes? One answer is that the para-athletes are not representative of the physically disabled community and produce a situational irony. What might be empowering for the individual para-athletes may be disempowering for the majority community as the awe of the remarkable reduces the respect for the ordinary. In a way, the Para-games might be viewed from a Goffmanian perspective as a genre of 'covering', a technique identified by Goffman (1963) to render more socially acceptable 'abominations of the body'. The de-emphasis of disability creates a distance from individuals with disabilities (Smith & Sparkes, 2008). This could accentuate stigmatisation of the larger community. Goffman (1963) writes:

> 'The Greeks, who were apparently strong on visual aids, originated the term stigma to refer to bodily signs designed to expose something unusual and bad about the moral statues of the signifier. The signs were cut or burnt into the body and advertised that the bearer was a slave, a criminal, or a traitor a blemished person, ritually polluted, to be avoided, especially in public places. Later, in Christian times, two layers of metaphor were added to the term: the first referred to bodily signs of holy grace that took the form of eruptive blossoms on the skin; the second, a medical allusion to this religious allusion, referred to bodily signs of physical disorder. Today the term is widely used in something like the original literal sense but is applied more to the disgrace itself than to the bodily evidence of it' (p.5).

Throughout modern history, the body has acted as an identity signifier and the imperfect have been prone to stigmatisation. Stigma refers to a characteristic that is considered a deformity perhaps leading to shame and discredit. A person in this sense is deemed as 'not quite human' (Goffman, 1963, p.7). Hence, covering is a form of tension management for visible and apparent stigma in order to remove potential exclusion and devaluation as a result of physical deformity. There is a negative result of the 'covering' role that the Paralympics might play. The reference to Aiden and McCarthy's (2014) study above points perhaps to this. To exemplify it further, China received a tally of 239 medals at Rio 2016 Paralympics, yet not long afterwards, China's State Council legislated the promotion of the abortion of fetuses with disabilities (Coonan, 2016). This ambiguity questions the meaning of the Paralympics and its value as a socialising tool for empowerment and inclusivity.

The focus on physical difference as a problem is said to stem from the authority of the Medical Model of Disability. This conceives disability as biological in nature and emphasises the authority of the medical profession (Addelson, 1983). The medical gaze, according to Foucault (1973) is 'that of a doctor supported and justified by an institution, endowed with the power of decision and intervention' (p.89). The discourse of the physically disabled as burdens (Brisenden, 1986; Drake, 1999) is said to stem from this. For example, the wheelchair is often associated as an aid rather than a vehicle for empowerment (Ashton-Shaeffer et al. 2001). As Brittain (2010) argues, the medical model 'colours people's perception of the validity of sport for disabled as 'real' sport' (p. 3). Consequently, the Paralympics is a 'marginal, deviant sports event as opposed to an elite sport competition involving athletes' (Purdue, 2013, p. 392). In this respect, it is questionable if it is a positive source of empowerment.

Further, there have been oppositional attitudes reported towards the para-athlete because of the medical model. Van Hilvoorde and Landeweerd (2008) point out that:

> 'There seems to be a sharp contrast between the athlete as a cultural hero and icon and the disabled person that needs extra attention or care; the one incorporating the peak of normality, human functioning at its best, the other often representing the opposite' (as cited in Smith, 2016, p. 20).

The above examples point to a clear division, at micro and macro levels, between the way para-athletes and their disability as well as para-athletes and the physically disabled community at large are viewed and treated. Thus, stigma exists as an internalised and structural phenomenon. In fact, the Paralympian as cultural hero and icon may also lead to the label of 'super-able' (Davis, 2014). The Paralympics might be forging what has become known as the supercrip iconography (de Silva & Howe, 2012) and this narrative may be developing as a stereotype. According to Berger (2004), supercrips are 'those individuals whose inspirational stories of courage, dedication, and hard work prove that it can be done, that one can defy the odds and accomplish the impossible' (as cited in Howe, 2008, p. 135). The Rio 2016 Paralympics Trailer, "We're the Superhumans" (2016) is one example. Elite Paralympians are framed as performing extraordinarily and producing heroic deeds. This is often simultaneously portrayed with narratives of personal tragedy overcome through great hardship with the end result that the athlete is no longer a burden. In this light, the media may be viewed as reinforcing the 'supercrip' narrative and aiding in the construction of this new stereotype. This may have negative socialising consequences for the larger community. Kama (2004) posits:

> 'Successful disabled people are put on a pedestal for their demonstrated ability to triumph. This triumph is used to validate the disabled individual and to alter societal perceptions. Consequently, the wish to see disabled who

'have done it' is particularly intense while the pitiful disabled trigger antipathy because they reproduce and reinforce disabled people's inferior positionality and exclusion' (p. 447).

The commonly physically disabled person may now have a standard which is difficult, if not impossible to achieve and this may be a continual underlying pressure on the general disabled community.

From the perspective of the para-athlete, it might also produce what has been termed as the Paralympic Paradox (Purdue & Howe, 2012). Purdue and Howe (2012) explain how the para-athlete plays two conflicting roles with the growth of the Paralympic movement. Making the Paralympics a globally-viewed event is seen as an important development. With the growth of performance and the development of independence, there is a deemphasis of the disability and a reduction of stigmatisation. This might lead to a greater acceptance by the non-disabled community of the para-athlete. However, simultaneously, there is a process of embodiment alienation occurring. In other words, the more para-athletes are accepted by the abled-bodied community, the more those athletes are distanced from the disability community. The resulting effect might be that the para-athlete loses credibility as a role model for the disabled community. The fact that prosthetics are extremely costly also accentuates this message. In 2018, the cost of one basic prosthetic leg is minimum $10,000 US dollars and up to $70,000 for one controlled by muscle movements (http://health.costhelper.com/prosthetic-legs.html). Para-athletes themselves may receive sponsorships but the general population is unlikely to have access to the latter. The cost of treatment is important. The socio-economic status of the physically disabled community is low. According to the U.S. Department of Labor's (2017) Office of Disability Employment Policy, people with disabilities in employment, aged 16 and over, is only 20.1% (https://www.apa.org/pi/ses/resources/publications/disability.aspx). People without disabilities of the same age range is 68.6%. This is a common pattern across the globe.

Intersectionality, and how ethnicity is related, is also very important in understanding the plight of the physically disabled. Ali et al. (2001) point out that the Disability Movement in Britain is led by white, middle-class, heterosexual, males and this may impact understanding of the difficulties faced by people with physical disabilities of minority cultures. Hill (1994) argues that a Black disabled man's experience is different. Ali et al. (2001) conclude the same with regards to Blacks and Asians. Their experiences of disability are different as they also deal with individual and institutional racism, both at school and the workplace. Further, their knowledge about services available to them is low and this limits access. Researchers point out that this leads to a very low self-image (Ali et al. 2001; Begum et al., 1994; Bignall & Butt, 2000) impacting the number of physically-disabled from different ethnicities in the para-games. Double British Paralympic medalist Kadeena Cox reported that she hoped to make her bronze in the T38 100m and gold in cycling's C4-5-time trial win in Rio inspire her fellow Black athletes. In an interview, she observed: 'I am in a small minority as a Black female with a disability' (Hope, 2016). Indeed, in the 2012

Guardian's Data Blog, it was found that the proportion of athletes from Black and other ethnic minorities on the British team was only 6%.

In the same way, gender is an issue in para-sport. In a 2018 paper, Brooke points out how Singaporean para-women athletes tend to be overrepresented in passive poses outside of the sporting arena. This is reconfirmed by Smith and Thomas (2005) in the British media. Para-sport is also viewed as a *primary masculinity-validating experience* (Dubbert, 1979, p. 164). It helps to consistently construct 'a male-created homosocial cultural sphere' that provides men with a 'psychological separation from the perceived feminisation of society while also providing dramatic symbolic proof of the *natural superiority* of men over women' (Messner, 1988, p. 200). The combination of these forces has led to the conclusion that female disabled athletes undergo a form of 'double jeopardy' (Hargreaves & Hardin, 2009). Hall (1996) also argues that female para-athletes are often viewed as 'sexually different' (as cited in Hargreaves & Hardin, 2009) in contrast to biological norms. Studies extending this work have concluded that female disabled athletes are often stereotyped as asexual (Richard, Joncheray, & Dugas, 2017). These authors cite Zitzelsberger (2005):

> 'Discourses of women with disabilities as non-gendered, nonsexual, childlike and dependent extend to assumptions regarding women being unable to be sexual, spouses, partners or mothers. Noticeable body differences cause confusion and comment' (cited in Richard, Joncheray, & Dugas, 2017, p. 64).

As Haraway (1991) argues, the artificial and biological deconstruct gender to produce an asexual narrative for the disabled woman (p. 178).

To conclude, there is evidence that the Paralympics may be an impactful tool as it does empower the para-athletes from across the globe. The non-disabled view people with disabilities as able through their sporting achievements. However, it cannot be viewed as a panacea for society's prejudices and negative perceptions towards individuals with disabilities. The disabled community seems to also be disempowered by the movement as Paralympians are given superhuman identity, which can be counterproductive. It is not wholly clear if the stigmatisation of the general disabled public has decreased. Individuals with disabilities seem to still be devalued and disempowered. Further, the para-athletes themselves might be living a form of paradox through their sport participation as it accentuates the 'supercrip' narrative which is thought to impede equality for all (Silva & Howe, 2012). As a benchmark for all disabled participating in sport, this is an ideology of exclusivity making 'failures' of those who cannot live up to expectations (Silva & Howe, 2012). The disabled/disabled binary may be increasing, which may lead to further Othering of the general disabled community (Silva & Howe, 2012). In that case, this could result in negative socialisation through sport.

The Paralympics could be a medium for change for the physically-disabled community as nations compete to demonstrate their inclusive practices. Also, it is clear that the Paralympic movement has its origins as an advocacy body. However, with the rise in mediatisation of the movement, and the para-athlete as cultural hero and icon, there may be an increase in the 'super-able' (Davis, 2014) persona. This could lead to further Othering of the disabled community who are not able to live up to the same standards. Thus, cultivating further the Paralympic Paradox. It is important that the movement has a positive impact at the ground level for the physically-disabled majority, not just those elites who compete. For this, more financial support and out-reach programmes to encourage sport participation are necessary. Intersectionality, in particular, ethnicity and gender, are also pressing issues in this field. Awareness-raising and effective policies on the ground to encourage more athletes from minority cultures are needed. Additionally, the media should strive to break away from the prevalence of either presenting passive images or asexual representations of female para-athletes. With these kinds of changes, some progress could be made.

REFERENCES

Addelson, K. P. (1983). "The man of professional wisdom". In S. Harding & M. B. Hintikka (Eds.), *Discovering reality* (pp. 165-186). Boston: Reidel.

Aiden, H. & McCarthy, A. (2014). "Current attitudes towards disabled people". *SCOPE*. Retrieved from http://www.scope.org.uk/Scope/media/Images/ Publication%20Directory/Current-attitudes-towards-disabled-people.pdf? ext=.pdf

Ali, Z., Fazil, Q., Bywaters, P., Wallace, L., & Singh, G. (2001). Disability, ethnicity and childhood: a critical review of research. *Disability & Society, 16*(7), 949-967.

Ashton-Shaeffer, C., Gibson, H., Holt, M., & Willming, C. (2001). "Women's resistance and empowerment through wheelchair sport". *World Leisure Journal, 43*(4), 11-21.

Beacom, A. (2018). "The Paralympic Movement and Diplomacy: Centring Disability in the Global Frame". In *the Palgrave Handbook of Paralympic Studies* (pp. 345-367). Palgrave Macmillan, London.

Beacom, A., & Brittain, I. (2016). "Public diplomacy and the international Paralympic committee: Reconciling the roles of disability advocate and sports regulator". *Diplomacy & Statecraft, 27*(2), 273-294.

Begum, N., Hill, M. & Stevens, A. (1994) Reflections: views of black people on their lives and community care, *CCETSW*, Paper 32.3 (Cambridge, Black Bear Press).

Berger, R. J. (2004). "Pushing forward: Disability, basketball, and me". *Qualitative inquiry, 10*(5), 794-810.

Bostrom, N. (2003). *The Transhumanist FAQ A General Introduction Version 2.1*. Retrieved from http://www.transhumanism.org/resources/FAQv21.pdf

———. (2005). "In defense of posthuman dignity". *Bioethics, 19*(3), 202–14.

———. (2005). "Ethical Issues for the 21st Century", ed. Frederick Adams (Philosophical Documentation Center Press, 2003); *Review of Contemporary Philosophy*, Vol. 4.

Bostrom, N. & Ord, T. (2006). "The Reversal Test: Eliminating Status Quo Bias in Applied Ethics", *Ethics 116*(4), 656-679.

Brisenden, S. (1986). "Independent living and the medical model of disability". *Disability, Handicap & Society, 1*(2), 173-178.

Brittain, I. (2004). "Perceptions of disability and their impact upon involvement in sport for people with disabilities at all levels". *Journal of Sport and Social Issues, 28*(4), 429-452.

———. (2010). *The Paralympic Games explained*. London: Routledge.

Brooke, M. (2018). The Singaporean Paralympics and Its Media Portrayal: Real Sport? Men-Only? *Communication & Sp*ort, 6(5), 1-20. 2167479518784278.

Coonan, C. (2016). "Paralympic success challenges China's attitude to disability". *The Irish Times*. Retrieved from https://www.irishtimes.com/news/world/asia-pacific/paralympic-success-challenges-china-s-attitude-to-disability-1.2813993

Cull, N. (2010). "Written evidence to House of Commons Select Committee (10 Nov. 2010)". *FCO public diplomacy: the Olympics and Paralympic Games 2012*. Response by Cull. Great Britain: Parliament. Retrieved from https://publications.parliament.uk/pa/cm201011/cmselect/cmfaff/581/581.pdf

Davis, R. (2014). "Oscar Pistorius and the Paradox of the Disabled Super-athlete". *Daily Maverick. South Africa.*

Donnelly, L. (2012). *Oscar Pistorius makes Olympic history*. Telegraph UK. Retrieved from http://www.telegraph.co.uk/sport/olympics/london-2012/9450469/Oscar-Pistorius-makes-Olympic-history.html

Drake, R. F. (1999) *Understanding disability politics*. London: MacMillan.

Dubbert, J. L. (1979). *A man's place: Masculinity in transition*. Englewood Cliffs, NJ: Prentice-Hall.

Foucault, M., (1973). "The Birth of the Clinic". *An Archaeology of Medical Perception*, London: Routledge.

The Guardian. What have we learned from the Paralympic Games? https://www.theguardian.com/sport/2012/sep/08/paralympics-what-have-we-learned

Gethins, M. (2014). *Para-athletes Push Prosthesis Innovations in Wide Range of Sports*. Canada: Medtronic.

Goffman, E. (1959). *The Presentation of Self in Everyday Life*. NY: Doubleday anchor books.

————. (1963) "Stigma". *Notes on Management of Spoiled Identity*. London: Penguin.

Hargreaves, J. A., Hardin, B. (2009). Women wheelchair athletes: Competing against media stereotypes. *Disability Studies Quarterly*, 29. Retrieved from http://www.dsq-sds.org/article/view/920/1095

Hill, M. (1994) 'They are not our Brothers': the disability movement and the black disability movement, in N. Begum, M. Hill & A. Stevens (Eds) *Reflections: views of black disabled people on their lives and community care*. CCET SW, Paper 32.3 (Cambridge, Black Bear Press).

Hope, N. (2016). Rio Paralympics 2016: Kadeena Cox aims to inspire black athletes. *BBC Sport*. https://www.bbc.com/sport/disability-sport/37331510

Howe, D. (2008). *The cultural politics of the Paralympic movement: Through an anthropological lens*. Routledge: UK.

Kama, A. (2004). "Supercrips versus the pitiful handicapped: Reception of disabling images by disabled audience members". *Communications*, 29(4), 447-466.

Lundberg, N., Bennett, J., & Smith, S. (2011). "Outcomes of adaptive sports and recreation participation among veterans returning from combat with acquired disability". *Therapeutic Recreation Journal, 45*(2), 105-120.

Messner, M. A. (1988). Sports and male domination: The female athlete as contested ideological terrain. *Sociology of Sport Journal*, 5, 197–211.

Persson, M. (2017). Aimee Mullins. Retrieved from http://iconmagazine.se/portfolio/aimee-mullins/

Purdue, D. (2013). "An (In) convenient Truce? Paralympic Stakeholders' Reflections on the Olympic-Paralympic Relationship". *Journal of Sport & Social Issues*, 37(4), 384-402.

Purdue, D. E. J., & Howe, P. D. (2012). "See the sport, not the disability: exploring the Paralympic paradox". *Qualitative research in sport, exercise and health*, 4(2), 189-205.

Roco & Bainsbridge, W. (2003). *Converging Technologies for Improving Human Performance: Nanotechnology, Biotechnology, Information Technology and Cognitive Science*. Kluwer Academic Publishers, Dordrecht Hardbound. Retrieved from http://www.wtec.org/ConvergingTechnologies/Report/NBIC_report.pdf1-4020-1254-3

Silva, C. F. & Howe, P. D. (2012). "The (in) validity of supercrip representation of Paralympian athletes". *Journal of Sport and Social Issues, 36*(2), 174-194.

Smith, B. (Ed.). (2016). *Paralympics and disability sport*. Routledge: UK.

Smith, B., & Sparkes, A. C. (2008). "Changing bodies, changing narratives and the consequences of tellability: A case study of becoming disabled through sport". *Sociology of health & illness*, *30*(2), 217-236.

Smith, A., & Thomas, N. (2005). The 'inclusion'of elite athletes with disabilities in the 2002 Manchester Commonwealth Games: An exploratory analysis of British newspaper coverage. *Sport, Education and Society*, *10*(1), 49-67.

Van Hilvoorde, I., & Landeweerd, L. (2008). "Disability or extraordinary talent—Francesco Lentini (three legs) versus Oscar Pistorius (no legs)". *Sports Ethics and Philosophy, 2*(2), 97-111.

Wolbring, G. (2012). "Expanding ableism: Taking down the ghettoization of impact of disability studies scholars". *Societies, 2*(3), 75-83.

———. (2008a). "Is there an end to out-able? Is there an end to the rat race for abilities?" *Media and Culture*, 11 (3). Retrieved from http://www.journal.media-culture.org.au/index.php/mcjournal/article/view/57

———. (2008b). "The politics of ableism". *Development, 51*(2), 252–258.

———. (2008c). "Why NBIC? Why human performance enhancement?" *The European Journal of Social Science Research, 21*(1), 25–40.

CHAPTER 9

Women Who Fight

During the renaissance of the Olympics, Baron Pierre de Coubertin, in 1896, declared:

> 'No matter how toughened a sports woman may be, her organism is not cut out to sustain certain shocks' (as reported in Casselbury, 2017)

De Coubertin thought it inappropriate for women to compete. Consequently, they did not in the first modern Olympic Games in 1896. By the 1970s, rigorous events like the Olympic Marathon were firmly established but women were still not competing nor were they running long distance competitions such as the 3000 metres before the 1980s. Women collapsing after some distance races, such as the 800-metre event, as men were doing also, led (male) Olympic organisers to hypothesise that this activity was too grueling for women. These words and events demonstrate how engrained patriarchal ideology truly is in sport; its origins are socio-culturally-oriented but justified with some biologically-focused argumentation as well.

Traditional gender norms continue to be channeled through sport through patriarchal structures (Channon, 2014; Channon & Jennings, 2014; Kavoura et al. 2017). Salaries and sponsorships are unequally distributed. Beatrice Frey, sport partnership manager at UN Women stated:

> 'I cannot think of any other industry that has such a wage gap, really. Depending on country context and sport, a man can be billionaire and a woman [in the same discipline] cannot even get a minimum salary' (cited in Perasso, 2017).

Media attention is unequivocally given to men's sport while women's sport is under-represented and trivialised (Kay, 2003; Kay & Jeanes, 2008). For example, in 2014 SportsCenter, an ESPN media programme, covered women's sport as only 2% of its total airtime (Cooky, Messner, & Musto, 2015). If the media does cover women, it is often in the form of aesthetic sport with a focus on grace and flexibility (Kay, 2003; Kay & Jeanes, 2008; Channon, 2014; Channon & Jennings, 2014; Glogower, 2009). Additionally, women are unquestionably more consistently referred to as 'girls' than men are 'boys'; and they tend to be called 'ladies' far more than men are 'gentlemen' (Koivula, 1999). This is part of the processes of infantilising and constructing docile passive bodies through patriarchal language. The male body as weapon is also consistently portrayed in the media through images of hits performed in contact sports such as the NFL. These images of male athletes seek to 'glorify their strength and power, even their violence' (Anleu, 2006, p. 370). Pronger's (2010) conclusion from his research on phallocentrism in sport is that homophobia and heterosexism are inextricably linked to competitive sport:

> 'Competitive sport produces a set of binaries that emanate from the traditional homophobic construction of desire: winner/loser, top/bottom, dominant/submissive, phallus/asshole. And these binaries have their fundamental logic in the patriarchal construction of masculine/feminine as the proper dispositions of men and women, respectively' (p. 171).

Gender marking is another example of a patriarchal structure for domination. It makes the male sporting realm the benchmark or standard and the female event, the 'Other'. The all-female rather than the open tournament moniker is a form of gender marking akin to that in other sports such as football with the World Cup and the Women's World Cup (Fink, 2015). The reason for this distinction appears to relate to the fact that there is a great difference in the perceived level of achievement attained and the prestige of a victory in an open rather than an all-female competition. It is a way to demean and marginalise women as athletes. In so doing, the stereotypical hegemonic status of males in sport is stressed as notions of difference enable males to construct a sense of identity and exclusivity (Yao, Mahood & Linz, 2010).

The forces of history and the patriarchal structures explored above result in the formation of the social world we know; one summed up effectively by Young (2005):

> 'The culture and society in which the female person dwells define woman as Other, as the inessential correlate to man, as mere object and immanence' (p. 31).

The social world has been partly constructed through what Connell (1987) refers to as 'body-reflexive practices'. She states:

> 'Body-reflexive practices...are not internal to the individual. They involve social relations and symbolism; they may well involve large-scale institutions. Particular versions of masculinity [and femininity] are constituted in their circuits as meaningful bodies and embodied meanings. Through body-reflexive practices, more than individual lives are formed: A social world is formed' (p. 64).

These body-reflexive practices enable and perpetuate the omnipresence of the male gaze and force women to 'do gender' (West & Zimmerman, 2009) and to behave in accordance to social expectations. As Merleau-Ponty (1962) tells us, the body is not only 'an object of the world, but our means of communication' (p.92) with it. It is simultaneously a product of our self-identity and the vehicle for its presentation. Thus, women act according to social expectations. West and Zimmerman (1987) declare that:

'Doing gender means creating differences between girls and boys and women and men, differences that are not natural, essential, or biological. Once the differences have been constructed, they are used to reinforce the 'essentialness' of gender' (p. 137).

As such, Coakley's (2009) notion of *power and performance* sport culture and the body as machine (Hoberman, 2001) and weapon (Messner, 1990) have traditionally been related to the realm of men's sports. However, in their paper, Roth and Basow (2004) refer to literature that demonstrates that men are only approximately 10% larger than women on average (p. 248). Roth and Basow (2004) also present Gutmann's study on one in four women who were able to lift 100lbs. They then question that, if these are the facts, women cannot be considered naturally weak. In Freedson's (1994) study, women leg-pressed 110% of what males could per kilogram of body mass. In this light, the notion of women's weakness appears to be a socially-constructed myth.

Women's mixed-martial arts (WMMA) stars, such as Ronda Rousey, might be said to be helping to break down these barriers by physically and symbolically challenging hegemonic masculinity; just as Roberta Gibb in 1966 did by clandestinely running the Boston marathon in an unofficial time of 3:21:25 and beating a large number of males. The sport of MMA, one which is also prone to a gender moniker as football is (Women's MMA), may be helping to bring women out of the Spiral of Silence (Noelle-Neumann, 1974) and empower them, and in so doing, empower the female gender. From the perspective of Mead's Symbolic Interactionism, women who fight might have symbolic powerful identities. In this chapter, the question explored pertains to whether these athletes are indeed empowering themselves and their gender through their sport and transcending the gender order tradition or whether they are actively consenting to the glass ceiling provided by the male gaze (Connell & Messerschmidt, 2005).

Over 150 countries and around a billion households worldwide interests itself in The Ultimate Fighting Championship (UFC) and MMA. As of the end of the 2017 season, the UFC had held over 400 events. It is now an established multibillion-dollar sport and boasts over 2 million Facebook likes. In 2013, the UFC signed the first female martial artist, Ronda 'Rowdy' Rousey. Rousey's fight with Zingano in February 2015 for the Bantamweight Championship of the World held at the Staples Centre, Los Angeles, California was the main event of the evening. According to Glogower (2009), Rousey's fighting displays might be a genre of gender-neutralisation: performing in a traditionally-male oriented activity and demonstrating power, aggression and courage. Further, Jakubowska, Channon and Matthews (2016) recently found that Polish WMMA star, Jędrzejczyk, also known as Joanna Violence, received significant media coverage with no attempts to sexualise the fighter. At present, in Poland, Jędrzejczyk is winning the hearts and minds of the Polish people. Her fights with Claudia Gadelha have been reviewed in Forbes (https://www.forbes.com/sites/brianmazique/2016/07/09/joanna-jedrzejczyk-vs-claudia-gadelha-results-performance-of-the-night-winners-and-highlights/

#4cd4d6249390), and WMMA fights are today starting to be discussed as big events in the most popular sports media such as ESPN.

It is possible, using a physical feminist perspective, to argue that women who fight are gradually 'undoing' gender and removing gender stereotypes and challenging patriarchal ideology that they are weak through sport (McCaughey, 1997; Roth & Basow, 2004); and perhaps socializing other women to become involved in the sport also. Physical feminism as a movement increased because physical strength as empowerment had been overlooked (McCaughey, 1997). Through developing physical strength, McCaughey (1997) suggests that women can be enabled. Further research concurs that gendered embodiment, and the experience of force and power, is enabling (Theberge, 2003). Jakubowska, Channon and Matthews (2016) conclude that WMMA fighter Jędrzejczyk's success 'challenges the discursive construction of fighting as a masculine enterprise' (p. 424). One of the significant reasons that they discern this is because of the fighter's success. Jakubowska (2015), in an earlier work, also attributes ability to be a pivotal factor for empowerment. Jędrzejczyk's art is reported in vivid depictions of her dazed and bloodied opponents, accompanied by vivid prose describing the 'dominant' champion's cool prowess in 'massacring' them' (Jakubowska, Channon & Matthews, 2016, p. 425).

Both psychological and physical strength for women's empowerment are reported to be essential (Castelnuovo & Guthrie, 1998; DeWelde, 2003; Roth & Basow, 2004; Velija et al. 2013). Castelnuovo and Guthrie (1998), McCaughey (1997) and DeWelde (2003) accentuate the importance of women being trained to overcome the fear of pain. Preconceived notions of weakness and vulnerability can be resisted and problematised in this way to develop a feminist awareness. It is evident that the type of media coverage WMMA receives differs considerably to the traditional one of weakness and passivity in women's sports. However, despite the positive accounts above, Jakubowska et al. (2016) argue that sexism cannot be subverted if there is no coverage of the women fighting. As with other women's sports, it remains at low market value in comparison to men's MMA (Jakubowska, Channon & Matthews, 2016). Although WMMA is increasing in popularity, the sport tends to remain a part of the 'male preserve' (Matthews, 2015). Additionally, Velija et al.'s (2013) and Castelnuovo and Guthrie (1998)'s research has demonstrated that the feminist consciousness is not necessarily present in martial arts. After Velija et al.'s (2013) study of several WMMA gyms in the United Kingdom, they conclude:

> 'It appears through the narratives of the women in this study that it is possible to be individually empowered by physical and mental strength, yet on the other hand, the women do not question dominant notions of gendered embodiment that position women's bodies as weaker than male bodies as they naturalise and accept that male strength ensures they are better suited to the sport' (p. 538).

Personal autonomy, the right to do what they wish, is viewed as the goal of the fighters in Velija et al.'s (2013) research. Additionally, some participants seek a slender and light body. Velija et al. (2013) question whether undoing gender occurs through women who fight because of this. It is possible that without the feminist mindset, the gender norms may prevail. This can also be linked to Longwe's notion of conscientisation as part of her Women's Empowerment Framework (as presented in March, Smyth, & Mukhopadhyay, 1999). Longwe points out that it is important to raise women's awareness that they may themselves contribute to their own discrimination through 'active consent' (Gramsci, 1971) of the gender order; and that the gender order needs to shift to a more egalitarian situation for change to occur. Similarly, according to Roth and Basow (2004), women can gain empowerment through sport provided that the intersubjectivity of body and mind is understood. In order for a 'feminist way of being' (Merleau-Ponty, 1962, p. 262) to develop, the mind-body construct needs to be committed to move beyond the male gaze (Mulvey, 2009). In the concluding section of their paper, Roth and Basow (2004) present the Mobius strip, an inverted three-dimensional figure eight from Elizabeth Grosz (1994). This figure can be viewed as a metaphorical representation of the mind-body construct. Grosz (1994) states that 'through a kind of twisting or inversion, one side becomes another' (p. 12). Through physical liberation, it is argued that it is possible to simultaneously strengthen the mind and reach mental liberation also. Both are said to affirm each other as they simultaneously develop. But both need to be developed for the 'feminist way of being' (Merleau-Ponty, 1962, p. 262) to take effect. This is confirmed by Velija et al. (2013) also who demonstrate that only with a feminist consciousness can change really be facilitated. In this context, the woman fighter's identity needs to be focused on transcending patriarchal ideology. However, if this is not the case, and if the fighter does not share these beliefs with other politicised women, she may be viewed as a rare phenomenon; the Other. These women may be seen as constructing a natural-born-fighter identity rather than a feminist one (Kavoura et al. 2017) and as deviant. This is said to have limited potential for generalisation to the female gender (Glogower, 2009) and thus little power for socialisation of other women into the movement. As Birrell (2000) states, these 'female athletes' are viewed as 'unnatural women' (p. 68). In Schippers' (2007) terminology, they are 'badasses' as they are muscular and aggressive. In this way, they are labelled as deviant and isolated, making them undesirables, and lack the potential to develop the processes of conscientisation (Longwe, as presented in March, Smyth, & Mukhopadhyay, 1999).

Ronda 'Rowdy' Rousey might be seen to challenge the victim narrative. However, she is still careful to be portrayed in a feminine way (Weaving, 2014), not wanting to be viewed as a 'badass' (Schippers, 2007). In 2012, Rousey was interviewed and photographed in *ESPN The Magazine*'s Body Issue. She wears pink hand wraps and, as Weaving (2014) states 'her lips are semi-parted, and it is as if there is a wind behind her gently blowing her long locks into perfect position' (p. 136). In the interview, Rousey claims: 'I'm like a Monet, from far away, I can look like a prissy model, but when you come closer you see the wear and tear of a fighter' (cited in Weaver, 2014, p.136). In 2016 Pantene's 'Strong is Beautiful' advert exclaimed 'Ronda Rousey shows that women contain multitudes—they can be strong, and beautiful, and whatever they want to be' (Monllos, 2016). This last statement from Monllos (2016) reflects the post-structural or neo-liberal feminist stance that women should have the freedom to express their sexuality freely without concern of critique. Jakubowska, Channon and Matthews (2016) are critical of this activity explaining that this kind of sexualisation is common in WMMA and can be also observed in campaigns from Gina Carano, Felice Herrig, Rin Nakai and Meisha Tate (p. 413). Guerandel and Mennesson (2007) also found that when in a mixed gender dojo, the gender stereotypes prevail. The women displayed their femininity through their dress and long hair. Using Cooley's (1998) Looking-Glass Self, these women might be said to construct their identity through socialisation processes by actively seeking to interpret what men might think about them and project that imagined judgement to create a virtual self. This guides their actions. Consequently, they seek to feminise themselves to undo the 'badass' (Schippers, 2007) characterisation (strong and aggressive) that they feel they might accumulate. Kavoura et al. (2017) conclude their research by stating that even with more women involved in martial arts today, the dominant discourses continue to maintain the narrative that women are 'biologically incapable of competitive judo' (p. 1) because aggression and strength are masculine traits. Therefore, little positive socialisation through WMMA may occur to undo gender.

These findings problematise empowerment through physical feminism and demonstrate that women who fight have to considerably negotiate the presentation of their identities in the media but also outside of the cage. This reveals the tensions that these women experience balancing their 'badass' (Schippers, 2007) characteristics with their femininity. However, if it is a femininity that is produced by the male gaze (Mulvey, 2009), it might not be constructive for the feminist cause to self-identify in that way.

It is clear that WMMA is impacting the way both men and women think about female gendered embodiment. It was only in 2004 that women's wrestling became an event at the Olympics, and even later, in 2012, for boxing. The 2020 Tokyo Olympics will see women's Karate events for the first time. These developments, along with the publicity that WMMA is garnering, might potentially play a pivotal role and socialise more women into environments where physical feminism can develop. Each year, it appears that more women are participating in female division bouts. For example, between 2014 and 2015, there was a 75 fight increase to 711 registered female fights. Moreover, in May 2018, UFC procured new U.S. media rights deals with Disney Direct-to-Consumer and International and ESPN Inc worth $300 million per-year. This will include the showing of 42 events on ESPN platforms per-year (Dwornik, 2018), demonstrating the potential reach the movement may have. However, as Velija et al.'s (2013) research confirms, fighting is possibly not enough. Women who fight might also need to build an ability to transcend their individual physical empowerment. It is argued that, if progress is to be made, these women should also cultivate a collective feminist consciousness recognizing the significance of their roles in changing traditional views of gendered embodiment and deconstructing the way that men's bodies alone are viewed as weapons (Velija et al. 2013). Activity, aggression, competition and strength are not masculine characteristics biologically. Similarly, passivity and weakness are not feminine characteristics biologically. These are traits developed over time as social constructs, of which sport plays an important role. Therefore, through participation in sport, it might be possible to help to work the other way and deconstruct these stereotypes. However, the right conditions in the media and outside the cage are required; along with the right feminist mindset. This way of seeing and being must be committed to move beyond the glass ceilings that men have constructed.

REFERENCES

Anleu, S. R. (2006). "Between Conformity and Autonomy". In K. Davis, M. Evans, & J. Lorber, J. (Eds.). *Handbook of Gender and Women's Studies*. Sage. (pp. 357-375).

Birrell, S. (2000). "Feminist theories for sport". In J. Coakley and E. Dunning. (Eds). *Handbook of Sports Studies*. London: Sage Publications. (pp. 61-76).

Casselbury, K. (2017). *Gender Discrimination in Sports*. Retrieved from https://www.livestrong.com/article/247625-gender-discrimination-in-sports/

Castelnuovo, S., & Guthrie, S. R. (1998). *Feminism and the female body: Liberating the Amazon within*. Boulder, CO: L. Rienner Publishers.

Channon, A. (2014). "Towards the undoing of gender in mixed-sex martial arts and combat sports". *Societies*, 4(4), 587-605.

Channon, A., & Jennings, G. (2014). "Exploring embodiment through martial arts and combat sports: A review of empirical research". *Sport in Society*, 17(6), 773-789.

Coakley, J. J. (2009). *Sports in Society: Issues and Controversies*. Edition, 10, McGraw-Hill Education.

Connell, R. (1987). *Gender and Power: Society, the Person, and Sexual Politics*. Stanford University Press.

Connell, R., & Messerschmidt, J. (2005). "Hegemonic Masculinity: Rethinking the Concept". *Gender and Society*, 19(6), 829-859.

Cooky, C., Messner, M. A., & Musto, M. (2015). "It's dude time! A quarter century of excluding women's sports in televised news and highlight shows". *Communication & Sport*, 3(3), 261-287.

Cooley, C. H., (1998). *Human Nature and the Social Order*. New York: Scribner's, 1902.

De Welde, K. (2003). "Getting physical: Subverting gender through self-defense". *Journal of Contemporary Ethnography*, 32(3), 247-278.

Dwornik, A. (2018). The Walt Disney Company's Direct to Consumer and International Segment and ESPN Reach Groundbreaking Agreement with UFC for Media Rights & Distribution. *ESPN Media Zone*, https://espnmediazone.com/us/press-releases/2018/05/the-walt-disney-companys-direct-to-consumer-and-international-segment-and-espn-reach-groundbreaking-agreement-with-ufc-for-media-rights-distribution/

Fink, J. S. (2015). "Female athletes, women's sport, and the sport media commercial complex: Have we really come a long way, baby?" *Sport Management Review*, 18(3), 331-342.

Freedson, P. (1994). "Muscle strength and endurance". *Women and Sport. Interdisciplinary Perspectives*. Champaign (USA), Human Kinetics.

Glogower, N. B. (2009). "A Good Defense Will Leave You Beautiful, a Bad Defense Will Make You Ugly: Gender in Muay Thai Kickboxing". *Master's Thesis*. America: University of Michigan.

Gramsci, A. (1971). *Selections from the Prison Notebooks of Antonio Gramsci*. Ed. and Transl. by Quintin Hoare and Geoffrey Nowell Smith. New York: International Publishers.

Guérandel, C., & Mennesson, C. (2007). "Gender construction in judo interactions". *International Review for the Sociology of Sport*, 42(2), 167-186.

Jakubowska, H. (2015). "Are women still the other sex: Gender and sport in the Polish mass media". *Sport in Society*, 18, 168-185.

Jakubowska, H., Channon, A., & Matthews, C. R. (2016). "Gender, media, and mixed martial arts in Poland: The case of Joanna Jędrzejczyk". *Journal of Sport and Social Issues*, 40(5), 410-431.

Kavoura, A., Kokkonen, M., Chroni, S. & Ryba, T. V. (2017). "Some women are born fighters: Discursive constructions of a Fighter's identity by female Finnish judo athletes". *Sex Roles*, 1-14.

Kay, T. (2003). "Sport and gender". *Sport and society: A student introduction,* 89-104.

Kay, T., & Jeanes, R. (2008). "Women, sport and gender inequity". *Sport and society: A student introduction,* 2, 130-154.

Koivula, N. (1999). "Gender stereotyping in televised media sport coverage". *Sex roles, 41*(7-8), 589-604.

March, C., Smyth, I. A., & Mukhopadhyay, M. (1999). *A guide to gender-analysis frameworks*. Oxfam: UK.

Matthews, C. R. (2016). "The tyranny of the male preserve". *Gender & Society, 30*(2), 312-333.

McCaughey, M. (1997). *Real knockouts: The physical feminism of women's self-defense*. NYU Press.

Merleau-Ponty, M. (1962). *Phenomenology of Perception*. Routledge & Kegan Paul.

Messner, M. A. (1990). "When bodies are weapons: Masculinity and violence in sport". *International review for the sociology of sport*, 25(3), 203-220.

Monllos, K. (2016). "Ad of the Day: Ronda Rousey Shows 'Strong is Beautiful' in This New Pantene Campaign". *Adweek*. Retrieved from http://www.adweek.com/brand-marketing/ad-day-ronda-rousey-shows-strong-beautiful-new-pantene-campaign-174984/

Mulvey, L. (2009). "Visual pleasure and narrative cinema" in Laura Mulvey, Laura, *Visual and other pleasures* (2nd ed.), Houndmills, Basingstoke, Hampshire England and New York: Palgrave Macmillan, pp. 14–30.

Noelle-Neumann, E. (1974). "The spiral of silence. A theory of public opinion". *Journal of Communication*, 24(2), 43–51.

Perasso, V. (2017). "100 Women: Is the gender pay gap in sport really closing?" *BBC News*. Retrieved from http://www.bbc.com/news/world-41685042.

Pronger, B. (2010). "Outta my Endzone: Sport and the territorial anus". In *Philosophical Perspectives on Gender in Sport and Physical Activity*, eds. P. Davis and C. Weaving, 160–77. London: Routledge.

Roth, A., & Basow, S. A. (2004). "Femininity, sports, and feminism: Developing a theory of physical liberation". *Journal of Sport and Social Issues, 28*(3), 245-265.

Schippers, M. (2007). Recovering the feminine other: Masculinity, femininity, and gender hegemony. *Theory and society*, *36*(1), 85-102.

Velija, P., Mierzwinski, M., & Fortune, L. (2013). "It made me feel powerful: women's gendered embodiment and physical empowerment in the martial arts". *Leisure studies, 32*(5), 524-541.

Weaving, C. (2014). "Cage fighting like a girl: Exploring gender constructions in the Ultimate Fighting Championship (UFC)". *Journal of the Philosophy of Sport, 41*(1), 129-142.

West, C., & Zimmerman, D. H. (2009). "Accounting for doing gender". *Gender & society*, 23(1), 112-122.

———. (1987). "Doing gender". *Gender & Society* 1(2), 125-51.

Yao, M. Z., Mahood, C., & Linz, D. (2010). "Sexual Priming, Gender Stereotyping, and Likelihood to Sexually Harass: Examining the Cognitive Effects of Playing a Sexually-Explicit Video Game". *Sex Roles*, 62(1-2), 77–88.

Young, I. M. (2005). *On female body experience: Throwing like a girl and other essays*. New York: Oxford University Press.

CHAPTER 10

Young Athletes and Character Development

Shields and Bredemeier (2001) point out that the 'sport builds character' narrative has created significant debate. Advocates argue that, through it, youth can learn qualities (Shields & Bredemeier, 1995). These include determination, emotional control, and fair-play as well as competitive and cooperative spirit. Skeptics point out however, that it is not necessarily true that these qualities are transferable outside of the sporting arena. They also report that aggression, violence and a win-at-all cost attitude might be more commensurate to competitive sport participation (Coakley, 2009). From these differing views, it is evident that sport may be considered as a positive or negative stimulant. In this chapter, we analyze socialisation through sport processes and specifically, the research linking sport to character development regarding young (7 to 12 years) and adolescent (12 to 17) athletes.

Weiss and Wiese-Bjornstal (2009) define positive youth development (PYD) as the growth of 'personal skills or assets, including cognitive, social, emotional, and intellectual qualities necessary for youth to become successfully functioning members of society' (p. 1). This growth should lead to 'optimal development' defined as:

> 'enabling individuals to lead a healthy, satisfying, and productive life, as youth and later as adults, because they gain the competence to earn a living, to engage in civic activities, to nurture others, and to participate in social relations and cultural activities' (Hamilton, Hamilton, & Pittman, 2004, p. 3).

Others conclude that PYD is based on the 5Cs (Lerner et al. 2005): competence, confidence, character, caring and connection. Competence is an ability to act well in a given domain; confidence, a feeling of self-worth; character, respect for others and social norms; and caring, empathy and compassion for others. The idea of 'relative plasticity' (Holt & Neely, 2011b, p. 301) is used to posit that human characteristics are malleable and able to change and develop throughout the life course. This concept is grounded in the positive psychology movement which seeks to nurture well-being (Snyder et al. 2002).

Often, proponents of this narrative, apply Social Control Theory (SCT) to support their claims. SCT contends that, when connected to others through traditional institutions as vehicles for social bonding, individuals are less likely to fall back to their natural propensity for deviance (Hirschi, 1969). For social control theorists such as Hirschi (1969), four elements to these institutions are necessary to prevent this degeneration: attachment, commitment, involvement, and belief. This latter relates to an individual's belief that the institutional rules have moral validity. Working with this type of theoretical perspective, much research has examined how sport participation may provide PYD (Bailey, 2006; Barber, Eccles, & Stone, 2001; Biddle, Sallis, & Cavill, 1998; Coalter, 2013; Eccles, Barber, Stone & Hunt, 2003; Eime, Young, Harvey, Charity, & Payne, 2013; Holt et al. 2011a; 2011b; McNeal 1995; Nichols et al. 2005; Richman & Shaffer, 2000). Holt et al. (2011a) report that sport participation is linked to developmental skills which spill over to other areas of youths' lives. For a group of 18 children (median age 12.5), these were 'emotional control, exploration, confidence, discipline and academic performance' (p. 494). Holt et al. (2008) in a study of Canadian high school soccer players, found that teamwork and leadership could be learned from team sport and transferred as a life skill. Similarly, Theberge (2000) reports camaraderie between women ice hockey players and a culture of inclusivity. Other developments uncovered are improvements in self-esteem, problem solving and goal setting (Barber, Eccles, & Stone, 2001). Nichols et al. (2005) found that sport led to PYD in terms of competence, coping and resilience. Shields and Bredemeier (1995) report how sportspersonship and fair play were developed. Biddle, Sallis, and Cavill, (1998) point out how sport can transform sedentary tendencies leading to better health and well-being. This has been substantiated more recently by Helgadottir et al. (2017). Social skills have also been found to benefit from sport participation (Holt et al. 2011a; 2011b; Nielsen et al. 2012). Finally, Putnam (1993) states that social capital can be acquired through sport within and across teams as well as across social strata. This leads to better relations and social status and to feelings of well-being. This was also verified by Welty Peachey et al. (2013) in their study of street football volunteers in the United States. They conclude that:

> 'volunteering fostered the preconditions for and actual social capital development by enhancing awareness and understanding about homelessness, building community and relationships with the homeless, enhancing passion to work in the social justice field, and developing self-satisfaction through a 'feel good' mentality' (p. 20).

Being involved as volunteers in street football enabled the homeless to derive satisfaction and reportedly led to a growth in their well-being.

Despite the positive connections so far presented, sport is not viewed as a panacea for youth problems. Giulianotti (2004) coined the term 'sport evangelists' to describe those who have constructed and perpetuated the generalised narrative that sport builds character. Anderson (2013) evidences this by citing from the *Encyclopedia of Mental Health*. Sport is said, in this reference work, to lead towards psychological wellbeing; it 'also affects other areas of human development, including moral development, social development, and career development' (p. 97). The etymology of these claims can be seen to relate to a tradition that began in the mid-1800s in England (Mangan, 1981 as cited in Sage, 1998, p. 15). Around this time, public schools for the ruling class started applying sport to enculture and instill discipline. The idea was for boys to prove themselves for the benefit of the British Empire (Sage, 1998). Sage also cites a well-known dictum from that time: 'The Battle of Waterloo was won on the playing fields of Eton' (p. 15). At this time, educational leaders viewed sport as a vehicle for nurturing citizenship. The slogan 'sport builds character' is still one that is heard in many settings. Yet, as Sage (1998) outlined two decades ago, 'there have been few well-conceived and implemented empirical research studies of the effects of organised sport involvement on the social development of young athletes' (p. 16). This is still reiterated today by a large number of skeptics.

In his paper 'Youth Sports: What Counts as Positive Development?' Coakley (2011) opposes that sport should solely be viewed for its 'essential goodness and purity'. He continues:

> 'Promoted and perpetuated by sport evangelists and kindred spirits, this belief inspires the strategy of using sports to create among young people the attributes needed to achieve personal success' (p. 306).

Coakley (2011) presents three effects related to these claims. The first is what he refers to as the 'fertilizer effect' (Coakley, 2011); this is that youth character development can be facilitated effectively through sport. The second is the 'guardian angel effect'. This is the narrative that sport participation can lead to success as it provides social and potential economic capital through relationships. The third is the 'car wash effect' (p. 308) or a cleansing of one's character. This refers to claims that sport can help change youth at risk. This segment of the population is said to benefit from sport as a strategy for rehabilitation through positive role modelling and moral education. It also prepares this youth to be civic-minded because it teaches them to respect the rules of the game. Following on from this, there are a great deal of studies rejecting the pro-PYD literature. A few of these studies are described here using Coakley's (2011) triadic typology.

Contrary to the PYD narrative, sport participation may cause serious anti-social behaviour. Opposing the 'fertilizer effect', value systems in aggressive sports are also likely to develop 'homophobia, sexism, racism, and ruthless competition' (Kreager, 2007, p. 706). Competition produces rivalry within a team (Brustad, Babkes, & Smith, 2001) as well as between teams (Siegenthaler & Gonzalez, 1997). Sport participation can also lead to use of performance enhancing substances (Dodge & Jaccard, 2006), alcohol and drug abuse (Lisha & Sussman, 2010), dating aggression (Forbes, Adams-Curtis, Pakalka & White, 2006) and extreme perfectionistic behaviour and criticality towards others' acts (Hill, Witcher, Gotwals, & Leyland, 2015). It also might lead to an over-adherence to authority (Anderson, 2013, p. 101). In a study of 106 children (9 to 12 years), researchers found that those involved in sports, possessed less moral reasoning than those who did not participate in sports (Bredemeier, Weiss, Shields, & Cooper, 1986). These authors posit that the level of contact in the sport is one of the clear causes for this observation. The literature linking sport participation to eating disorders amongst male and female athletes is also extensive (Nattiv et al. 2007; Smolak et al. 2000; Taub & Blinde, 1992). In sum, there appears to be a substantial amount of literature to negate the 'fertilizer effect' of the 'sport builds character' narrative.

Serious anti-social behaviour in sport may not represent strain (Merton, 1938) in society. Instead, it might reflect the sport ethic. The paradox presented by Hughes and Coakley (1991) is 'positive deviance'. This concept does not assume that deviance is natural human behaviour. It does not link social alienation to anomie or a lack of moral values. Hughes and Coakley (1991) argue that deviance in sport is actually a result of embracing the normative sport ethic. It is a socially-constructed modus operandi. The sport ethic in modern day sport competition is comprised of striving for distinction; sacrifice; playing through pain, and accepting no limits. Aggressive behaviour is valued even honoured as is the normalisation of pain. In Hughes and Coakley's (1991) paper, they hypothesise that it is this environment that has caused the growth of performance-enhancing drugs in sport; as athletes seek to push their boundaries on the field to achieve success, which is very much a finite resource.

Regarding the 'car wash effect' (Coakley, 2011), research from Kreager (2007) directly questions those who consider sport as vehicle for rehabilitation. The author concludes that involvement in contact sports is more likely to lead to the further development of aggression rather than reducing it. Kreager (2007) cites a United States' National Longitudinal Study of Adolescent Health which presents information that athletes of violent sports such as American football and wrestling are significantly more likely to become involved in serious violent fighting than those from other sports such as baseball, tennis and athletics. The effectiveness of the narrative that at-risk youths can learn to control their aggressive tendencies by following moral codes embued in aggressive sports is questioned by other authors also. Messner (1990) points out how winning is 'predicated on the successful utilisation of violence' (p. 203). Moreover, Gubbels et al. (2016) find that higher levels of anger and externalizing behaviours develop through contact sports. Similarly, Ziaee, Loftian, Amini, Mansournia & Memari (2012) conclude that 'judo training may have no influence on anger control' (p. 9).

Kay and Bradbury (2009) found that youth developed social capital in the community, but that sport was only one of multiple factors at play. This negates the 'guardian angel effect' (Coakley, 2011). Skinner et al. (2008) review several sport programmes in the UK, Australia, and Canada, and their potential in developing social capital for their participants. They conclude in the same way. The structure of the programmes, the way that they are organised, and the personality type of the individual, are all essential elements in building social capital. Similarly, research from Alegi (2000) on Black African workers and youth involved in football found that individuals were more motivated by personal mobility rather than developing social capital through new relations. In contrast to the 'guardian angel effect' (Coakley, 2011), Coakley (1992) uncovers an identity tunnel which tends to produce a 'one-dimensional identity' through sport. The more an athlete commits to a sport, the more his life is centred in that milieu. If only relations with others are built on athletic participation and achievements, the normative sport ethic becomes the significant identifier for the individual producing the one-dimensional identity. Lack of participation in other social environments may be restrictive in this sense as the type of social bonds are limited. Thus, it could be argued that sport participation narrows an athletes' social capital to only coaches and teammates (Nixon, 1996).

Researchers have also argued that it is competition itself that needs to be reconsidered for PYD. In 'Promoting Healthy Competition Using Modified Rules and Sports from Other Cultures', Constantinou (2014) suggests the modification of some traditional sports to promote what she calls 'healthy competition'. She does not fully condemn competitive sport but refers to Alfie Kohn's (1986) debunking of four myths about competition. Kohn (1986) argues that competitive sport in fact diminishes enjoyment and productivity and promotes ethically-unsound behaviour. He opts for cooperative sports without a zero-sum outcome. In contrast, Constantinou (2014) argues that competition can be healthy if it is related to 'true competition' (Shields & Bredemeier, 2010), that is 'striving with' rather than 'against' an opponent or team. To play at one's optimum level, it is important to have an opponent of similar ability. Through a cooperative striving with each other, each side is pushed to perform to their utmost abilities. When professional athletes strive to win at all costs and fail to exhibit positive values through acts such as match fixing or wanting to hurt their opponent, they are manifesting unhealthy competitive drives.

With the implications of this complex multiple-variant environment, it is evident that PYD is not necessarily an outcome from sport participation. The debate in this field of PYD leads Coakley (2011) to conclude that it is 'contingent' (p. 309). Exposure to a variety of sports and the possibility of developing other social networks outside of sport can be impactful. Fraser-Thomas, Coté and Deakin (2008) and Côté, Baker and Abernethy, (2007) posit that a balance of deliberate practice and play as well as exposure to several sports at early age can lead to a more effective development. The basic premise is that children involved in deliberate practice with limited time for play and little exposure to other sports may burn out and exit early from sport or develop one-dimensional identities, which might lead to deviant behaviour. Exposure to moral education as part of sport participation might also be helpful in PYD. Twemlow and Sacco (1998) present teaching of Karate with a philosophy linked back to the training of Samurais. As part of their skills development, Samurais traditionally received training in flower arranging and calligraphy. What might be termed 'sissy' sports were viewed as helping the Samurai to develop 'tenacity, endurance and patience' (p. 514). Similarly, Danish et al. (2005) point out that what seems clear from the literature, is that sport can teach life skills, but the key is how the programme is structured and delivered.

Some authors have thus listed out some of the necessary conditions to facilitate PYD. Holt et al. (2008) state that 'nothing magical about school sport will teach adolescents life skills' (p. 298). They list several contingent variables that can be related to whether sport will provide an avenue for PYD. These are the type of sport played; the influence of significant others; the culture of a sport and the environment in which it is practiced as well as how it is viewed by society; the social relations developed through the sport; the way the sport is integrated in the participant's life; and the changes that occur over the life course. In the same way, Lerner et al. (2005) conclude that youth programmes may promote the 5 Cs if they entail 'sustained adult-youth relationships; youth skill-building activities; and opportunities for youth participation in leadership of community-based activities' (as cited in Holt & Neely, 2011b, p. 307). Moreover, a study from the National Research Council and Institute of Medicine (2002) concluded that the optimal conditions for PYD are '(a) safe and health-promoting facilities, (b) clear and consistent rules and expectations, (c) warm, supportive relationships, (d) opportunities for meaningful inclusion and belonging, (e) positive social norms, (f) support for efficacy and autonomy, (g) opportunities for skill building, (h) coordination among family, school, and community efforts' (as cited in Holt & Neely, 2011b, p. 307). Further, Weiss and Wiese-Bjornstal (2009) conclude:

> 'A caring and mastery-oriented climate, supportive relationships with adults and peers, and opportunities to learn social, emotional, and behavioural life skills—these are the nutrients for promoting positive youth development through physical activity' (p. 7).

From these researchers' views, it is possible to observe that there are certain characteristics needed for a successful sport programme to build positive youth development. Anderson (2013) presents i9 sports as one youth sports movement that comprises some of these. This model, founded in 2003, is an American corporate franchise. It is consumer-based as it is privately managed, and the parents pay for their children's activities. The model needs to cater for customer demands to be successful. Anderson (2013) argues that because parents have more say in the way the programmes are run, these tend to put much more emphasis on safer non-contact sports; they also promote mixed gender teams, and strive to be more inclusive, sanctioning any forms of Othering. Finally, they engage in rotating players and coaches so that negative dynamics, between and within teams from recurrent competition, can be avoided. Hence, Anderson (2013) contends that it can be seen to represent cultural opposition to what we know of modern institutionalised sports.

To conclude, it is probable that the 'sport builds character' narrative is not entirely a given and should not be taken for granted. According to Hyman (2009), in the United States alone, approximately 41 million youths engage in organised team sports, yet as Anderson (2013) posits, parents know little about the real impact that traditional sport might have on their children. Anderson (2013) argues that the monolithic PYD message from 'Sport Evangelists' (Giulianotti, 2004) has politically significant ramifications. He points out how it might prevent public funding on research into sport, which might advocate changes to the institutional practices. Any significant challenges in these practices could impact the Ideological State Apparatus in place and demystify much of the structures related to gender, race, class, physical ability and cultural norms. Models such as the i9 experience seem to demonstrate that as parents have more of a say, many of them are inclined to seek practices that shift away from the hegemonic youth sport models. For Anderson (2013), it is probable that more inclusive practices will continue to develop but only as neo-liberal forms because parents are clients and have more control.

REFERENCES

Alegi, P. C. (2000). "Keep Your Eye on the Ball: A Social History of Soccer in South Africa", 1910-1976. *Doctoral dissertation*, Boston University, Boston.

Anderson E. (2013). "*I9* and the Transformation of Youth *Sport*". *Journal of* Sport *and Social Issues*, 37: 97-111

Bailey, R. (2006). "Physical education and sport in schools: A review of benefits and outcomes". *Journal of school health*, *76*(8), 397-401.

Barber, B. L., Eccles, J. S., & Stone, M. R. (2001). "Whatever happened to the 'Jock,' the 'Brain,' and the 'Princess'? Young adult pathways linked to adolescent activity involvement and social identity". *Journal of Adolescent Research*, 16, 429-455

Biddle, S. J., Sallis, J. F., & Cavill, N. (1998). *Young and active? Young people and health-enhancing physical activity-evidence and implications*. Health Education Authority.

Bredemeier, B. J., Shields, D. L., Weiss, M. R., & Cooper, B. A. (1986). "The relationship of sport involvement with children's moral reasoning and aggression tendencies". *Journal of Sport Psychology*, *8*(4), 304-318.

Brustad, R., Babkes, M., & Smith, A. (2001). "Youth in sport: Psychological considerations". In R. N. Singer, H. A. Hausenblas, & C. M. Janelle (Eds.), *Handbook of Sport Psychology* (2nd ed., pp. 604–635) New York: John Wiley.

Coakley, J. (1992). "Burnout among adolescent athletes: A personal failure or social problems?" *Sociology of Sport Journal*, 9, 271-285.

———. (2009). *Sports in Society: Issues and Controversies*. Edition, 10, McGraw-Hill Education.

———. (2011). "Youth sports: What counts as positive development?" *Journal of sport and social issues*, *35*(3), 306-324.

Coalter, F. (2013). "Game Plan and The Spirit Level: the class ceiling and the limits of sports policy?" *International journal of sport policy and politics*, *5*(1), 3-19.

Constantinou, P. (2014). "Promoting Healthy competition using modified rules and sports from other cultures". *Strategies*, *27*(4), 29-33.

Côté, J., Baker, J., & Abernethy, B. (2007). "Practice and Play in the Development of Sport Exercise". *Handbook of Sport Psychology*, Chapter 8, 184-202.

Danish, S. J., Petitpas, A., & Hale, B. (1995). "Psychological interventions: A life development model". In S. M. Murphy (Ed*.), Sport psychology interventions* (pp. 19-28). Champaign, IL; Human Kinetics Publishers.

Dodge, T. L., & Jaccard, J. J. (2006). "The effect of high school sports participation on the use of performance-enhancing substances in young adulthood". *Journal of adolescent health*, *39*(3), 367-373.

Eccles, J. S., Barber, B. L., Stone, M., & Hunt, J. (2003). "Extracurricular activities and adolescent development". *Journal of Social Issues*, 59, 965-889

Eime, R. M., Young, J. A., Harvey, J. T., Charity, M. J., & Payne, W. R. (2013). "A systematic review of the psychological and social benefits of participation in sport for children and adolescents: informing development of a conceptual model of health through sport". *International Journal of Behavioral Nutrition and Physical Activity*, *10*(1), 98.

Forbes, G. B., Adams-Curtis, L. E., Pakalka, A. H., & White, K. B. (2006). "Dating aggression, sexual coercion, and aggression-supporting attitudes among college men as a function of participation in aggressive high school sports". *Violence Against Women*, *12*(5), 441-455.

Fraser-Thomas, J., Cote, J., & Deakin, J. (2008). "Understanding dropout and prolonged engagement in adolescent competitive sport". *Psychology of Sport and Exercise,* (9), 645–662.

Giulianotti, R. (2004). *Sport and modern social theorists*. Springer. UK.

Gubbels, J., van der Stouwe, T., Spruit, A., & Stams, G. (2016). Martial arts participation and externalizing behaviour in juveniles: A meta-analytic review. *Aggression and Violent Behavior*, 28, 73-81.

Hamilton, S. F., Hamilton, M. A., & Pittman, K. (2004). "Principles for youth development". *The youth development handbook: Coming of age in American communities*, *2*, 3-22.

Helgadóttir, B., Owen, N., Dunstan, D. W., Ekblom, Ö., Hallgren, M., & Forsell, Y. (2017). "Changes in physical activity and sedentary behavior associated with an exercise intervention in depressed adults". *Psychology of Sport and Exercise*, *30*, 10-18.

Hill, A. P., Witcher, C. S. G., Gotwals, J. K., & Leyland, A. F. (2015). "A qualitative study of perfectionism among self-identified perfectionists in sport and the performing arts". *Sport, Exercise, and Performance Psychology, 4*(4), 237-253.

Hirschi, T. (1969). *Causes of Delinquency*. Los Angeles: University of California Press.

Holt, N. L., Tink, L. N., Mandigo, J. L., & Fox, K. R. (2008). "Do youth learn life skills through their involvement in high school sport?" A case study *Canadian Journal of Education/Revue canadienne de l'éducation*, 281-304.

Holt, N. L., Kingsley, B. C., Tink, L. N., & Scherer, J. (2011a). "Benefits and challenges associated with sport participation by children and parents from low-income families". *Psychology of sport and exercise*, *12*(5), 490-499.

Holt, N. L., & Neely, K. C. (2011b). "Positive youth development through sport: A review". *Revista iberoamericana de psicología del ejercicio y el deporte*, *6*(2).

Hughes, R., & Coakley, J. (1991). "Positive deviance among athletes: The implications of overconformity to the sport ethic". *Sociology of sport journal*, *8*(4), 307-325.

Kay, T., & Bradbury, S. (2009). "Youth sport volunteering: developing social capital?" *Sport, education and society*, *14*(1), 121-140.

Kohn, A. (1986). *No contest: The case against competition*. Boston: Houghton Mifflin.

Kreager, D. A. (2007). "Unnecessary roughness? School sports, peer networks, and male adolescent violence". *American sociological review*, *72*(5), 705-724.

Lerner, R. M., Almerigi, J. B., Theokas, C., & Lerner, J. V. (2005). "Positive youth development a view of the issues". *The journal of early adolescence*, *25*(1), 10-16.

Lisha, N. E., & Sussman, S. (2010). "Relationship of high school and college sports participation with alcohol, tobacco, and illicit drug use: A review". *Addictive behaviors*, *35*(5), 399-407.

McNeal Jr, R. B. (1995). "Extracurricular activities and high school dropouts". *Sociology of education*, 62-80.

Merton, R. K. (1938). "Social Structure and Anomie." *American Sociological Review*, 3: 672-82.

Messner, M. A. (1990). When bodies are weapons: Masculinity and violence in sport. *International review for the sociology of sport*, *25*(3), 203-220.

Nichols, G., Taylor, P., James, M., Holmes, K., King, L., & Garrett, R. (2005). "Pressures on the UK voluntary sport sector". *Voluntas: International Journal of Voluntary and Nonprofit Organizations*, *16*(1), 33-50.

Nicholls, S., Giles, A. R., & Sethna, C. (2011). "Perpetuating the 'lack of evidence'discourse in sport for development: Privileged voices, unheard stories and subjugated knowledge". *International review for the sociology of sport*, *46*(3), 249-264.

Nielsen, G., Grønfeldt, V., Toftegaard-Støckel, J., & Andersen, L. B. (2012). "Predisposed to participate? The influence of family socio-economic background on children's sports participation and daily amount of physical activity". *Sport in Society*, *15*(1), 1-27.

Nixon, H.L. (1996). The relationship of friendship networks, sports experiences, and gender to expressed pain thresholds. *Sociology of Sport Journal*, 13(1), 78-86.

Putnam, R. (1993). *Making Democracy Work: Civic Traditions in Modern Italy*. Princeton University Press, Princeton.

Richman, E. L., & Shafer, D. R. (2000). "If you let me play sports: How might sport participation influence the self-esteem of adolescent females?" *Psychology of Women Quarterly*, 24, 189-199.

Sage, G. (1998). "Does sport affect character development in athletes?" *Journal of Physical Education, Recreation & Dance, 69*(1), 15-18.

Shields, D. L. L., & Bredemeier, B. J. L. (1995). *Character development and physical activity*. Human Kinetics Publishers.

————. (2001). "Moral development and behavior in sport". *Handbook of sport psychology*, *2*, 585-603.

Siegenthaler, K. L., & Gonzalez, G. L. (1997). "Youth sports as serious leisure: A critique". *Journal of Sport and Social Issues*, *21*(3), 298-314.

Skinner, J., Zakus, D. H., & Cowell, J. (2008). "Development through sport: Building social capital in disadvantaged communities". *Sport management review*, *11*(3), 253-275.

Smolak, L., Murnen, S. K., & Ruble, A. E. (2000). "Female athletes and eating problems: A meta-analysis". *International journal of eating disorders*, *27*(4), 371-380.

Snyder, C. R., Lopez, S. J., Aspinwall, L., Fredrickson, B. L., Haidt, J., Keltner, D., & Wrzesniewski, A. (2002). *The future of positive psychology: A declaration of independence*.

Taub, D. E., & Blinde, E. M. (1992). "Eating disorders among adolescent female athletes: Influence of athletic participation and sport team membership". *Adolescence*, *27*(108), 833.

Theberge, N. (2000). *Higher goals: Women's ice hockey and the politics of gender*. SUNY Press.

Twemlow, S. W., & Sacco, F. C. (1998). The application of traditional martial arts practice and theory to the treatment of violent adolescents. *Adolescence*, *33*(131), 505-518.

Weiss, M. R., & Wiese-Bjornstal, D. M. (2009). *Promoting positive youth development through physical activity*. Retrieved from http://presidentschallenge.org/informed/digest/docs/september2009digest.pdf #

Welty Peachey, J., Cohen, A., Borland, J., & Lyras, A. (2013). "Building social capital: Examining the impact of Street Soccer USA on its volunteers". *International Review for the Sociology of Sport*, *48*(1), 20-37.

Ziaee, V., Lotfian, S., Amini, H., Mansournia, M., & Memari, A. (2012). Anger in adolescent boy athletes: A comparison among judo, karate, swimming and non-athletes. *Iranian Journal of Pediatrics*, *22*(1), 9-14.

Conclusion to Case Studies in Sport Socialisation and Future Cases

Throughout the book, we have examined processes of socialisation into, out of and through sport. This is a field that requires more attention in its own right. Currently, it only tends to appear as a chapter in a book (Coakley, 2009; Beedie & Craig, 2010; Delaney & Madigan, 2015; Leonard, 1998). By exploring socialisation, the analyst can investigate the tensions between structure and agency particularly in states where there is a strong ideological apparatus, or where capitalist market forces dictate behaviour; as well as the role that significant more intimate others play in determining a person's self-hood. Sport is a field that provides fascinating insights into these processes. It also plays an important role in identity construction and enables us to examine the intersections between gender, race, socio-economic status or class, physical ability and cultural norms. These are all inextricably linked to sport socialisation processes. Reasons for entering into, continuing in, and leaving sport, help the researcher to perceive ideologies in society and to understand the underlying reasoning and motivations behind participation in sport.

For socialisation into sport, we have studied processes at the macro, or governmental level as seen in China (Hong, 2004); and at the meso level, as seen in the Black African community in the United States (Beamon, 2010) as well as the corporate participation in adventure racing and dragon boating (Brooke, 2015; Kay & Laberge, 2002). For the section on socialisation out of sport, gender was the main theme under investigation. It was analyzed in three specific settings: within the female Muslim community; in women's eSports; and with regard to the difficulties faced by intersex athletes. The final section looked at socialisation through sport and how identity can be constructed over time through sport participation. For this, three cases were the focus: people with disabilities; women who fight; and positive youth development (PYD). In this final chapter, we recap on these studies and their implications. We then consider future topics for investigation in sport socialisation.

In the case study on child athletes in China, we explored how the institution pressurises individual into sport. The Chinese government has, over several decades now, maintained state ideology or an Ideological State Apparatus (Althusser, 1971) to ensure Olympic success by establishing sporting regimes to nurture athletes from an early age. This was explored and the consequences for child athletes socialised into this nation's sports schools analysed (Hong, 2004; Hong et al. 2005). Parents, often from poor socio-economic status, send their children to sports schools as an opportunity to acquire capital. However, according to human rights activists, it is questionable that a child be treated in this way. The documentary Little Big Dreams (https://www.youtube.com/watch?v=ZtS9RSPDpJs) from Nurture presents very clearly the kind of lives these young children lead. Long hours, brutal discipline and no opportunity to see family over long periods of time culminate in a very harsh environment. Government plays a major role in self-hood construction in China and it takes on a primary agent role as it socialises these would-be champions into these schools.

Family, neighbourhood, government, as well as the media and film, have also been seen to contribute a major role in sport socialisation. This was explored regarding Black African Americans' socialisation into sport (Beamon, 2010; Beamon & Bell, 2006; 2011) in the United States. This low socio-economic minority group is exposed to potential success through sport on several levels (Edwards, 2000). As a consequence, African American families and neighborhoods become sites for primary and significant secondary agents of socialisation. Beamon (2010) explains that the high levels of African American participation in sports, such as basketball and American football, are clearly due to ideological processes. This can mean a life of wealth for a tiny few, but the large majority drop out and often find themselves lacking any background for activities other than sport. Hoberman (1997) points out that this also creates 'a clan pride based on rejecting intellectual role models' (p. 3), which probably is a significant factor for the very poor levels in school achievement of African American males. They are consistently underperforming and are more likely to be expelled or to be classified as having a learning or emotional disability than Whites. Professor Shaun Harper, Director at the Center for the Study of Race and Equity in Education at the University of Pennsylvania, concluded in 2013 that young Black men made up 2.8% of undergraduate students in university but 57.1% of the men's football and 64.3% of the men's basketball teams. What is witnessed in this case is Cultural Reproduction in the Bourdieusian (1986) sense, systemically maintained through racial stacking in sport. In sum, there is a nexus of racial discrimination.

Finally, private institutions such as corporations can also have a major impact on socialisation into sport (Brooke, 2015; Kay & Laberge, 2002). Commonly, the corporate discourse presents, even mythologises, how corporate objectives may be engineered through sport. Synchronisation through effort and teamwork to maximise efficiency is the formula required for a successful team and institution. However, the effectiveness of the value engineering is questioned. Corporate workers involved in company sport may be socialised into participating for reasons contrary to the corporate objectives. For example, members might also join to relax from work or build friendships outside of the workplace. Other findings suggest that individuals might be involved in corporate sport for their own individual gain and status-building amongst their rivals at work; and this might be wholly contrary to the reasoning behind the corporate sporting culture. Consequently, the contradictions between structure and agency in this field are very interesting; in particular, in market-driven capitalist cultures.

It was noted in the introduction how gender is perhaps the most researched topic in sport socialisation. This is because, as Messner (1988) has argued, it is through sport that we learn how to do gender as it provides men with a 'psychological separation from the perceived feminisation of society while also providing dramatic symbolic proof of the *natural superiority* of men over women' (p. 200). For the section on socialisation out of sport, gender was the main theme under investigation. In the first chapter on Muslim women, it was the patriarchal and socio-economic structures, not the religious values that were presented, as the main reasons why women athletes remain vastly underrepresented in sport. In some Islamic communities such as Afghanistan, Pakistan and Saudi Arabia (Walseth, 2006), women often face brutal harassment. Their control is viewed as a necessary 'symbol of cultural maintenance' (Walseth, 2006, p. 91). The common argument in the media is that it is the hijab that socialises Muslim women out of sport. It was concluded that it might be an issue for some as the ethical hijab can be interpreted to prevent women entering the same water as non-Muslims. However, for many, the hijab is not an issue as sporting federations no longer ban head veils or full body hijabs; these are even available for swimming competitions today. The problem is clearly how the Islamic state Clerics interpret the hijab and use it as a tool to control women. Additionally, there was a brief exploration of why the number of Muslim women in developed nations might be low. In countries like the United Kingdom, there are few Muslim women and men in professional sport. In the UK, social mobility for Muslims is highly restricted. An upbringing in the lowest socio-economic areas of major cities means that money is an issue. For these men and women, time is needed to look for employment and to earn money for the household. Additionally, in these built-up urban areas, little infrastructure is given over for sport. This is in stark contrast to white middle class city and educational environments.

The second chapter in this section on socialisation out of sport explored the toxic hypermasculine environment of the eSports environment today and the discrimination against women that can be found there (Loebenberg, 2018). It was argued that the geek masculinity of this field of practice, and structures in place, result in gender discrimination and are causes for women's lack of presence (Taylor, 2012). According to Souvlis (as reported in Lane & Jackson, 2017), women make up less than 1% of the world's total eSports paid gamers and their remuneration considerably differs to that of men. This is despite the apparent potential for eSports to be mixed gender as it seemingly cannot justify itself to be proof of the natural superiority of men over women' (Messner, 1988, p. 200). In-game characters and advertisements for games commonly objectify and feminise women. Female gamers suffer frequent sexual abuse on Twitch live streams. This is added to by the out-of-game cosplay and doxxing that occurs at conventions. The treatment has led to what Noelle-Nuemann (1974) terms the Spiral of Silence (SOS) as many women strive to remain anonymous in the gaming world. Notwithstanding, some female gamers do persevere and often live stream on Twitch. One such star is YeoChoiMi, a Korean, Jazzzy and Missharvey, a North American, who has her own youtube channel (https://www.youtube.com/channel/UCHeiBDz6uo0v1EGnXyY7aVg). There are also advocacy bodies such as AnyKey who concentrate on developing the number of women in eSports. AnyKey helps to provide female gamers with financial support and encourage more women into the gaming industry. It was concluded that currently, a great deal of change is required in this field if more women are to participate.

The final chapter in this second section examined intersex athletes in sport and the access difficulties they experience. From an early age, children are socialised into learning appropriate male and female behaviour and homophily, and same-sex networks are developed (Messner, 2002). Sport is constructed around this binary and this means that intersex athletes face what many view as discrimination (Connell, 1987; Sullivan, 2011). As Foddy and Savulescu (2011) argue, 'gender is not a binary quantity' (p. 1184) and any form of segregation based on gender should be considered as an 'inconsistent and unjust policy'. This policy forces transgender athletes to conform to one or the other binary genders, which is not rational because athletes who do not are depicted as abnormal. Transgender athletes are thus often socialised out of sport. Example athletes were presented such as the South African 2009 World Track and Field Championships title winner, Caster Semenya, who was banned for 11 months from competing due to the supposed unfair advantage that her intersex identity gave her; and Indian, Dutee Chand, who was dropped from the 2014 Commonwealth Games because of the Athletic Federation of India's interpretation of her hyperandrogenism. It was argued in the chapter that this genre of treatment helps to confirm and promote hegemonic masculinity. As Sullivan (2011) contends, the unfairness narrative about transgender athletes such as Semenya, represents ideology constraining the female body's performance and structuring its form.

The final section looked at socialisation through sport and how identity can be constructed over time through sport participation for both those involved and the wider communities. The first chapter was about how people with disabilities negotiate stigma and whether through sport, they are empowered. We primarily explored how stigma, through the abominations of the body as a socialising force, can devalue and exclude people with disabilities because of their physical differences. This was even linked to government policy. For example, China, having been highly successful at the Paralympic Games of 2016, issued a national action plan to encourage the abortion of fetuses found to have disabilities, aiming to effectively reduce new disabilities by 2020 (The State Council, 2016). Further, much work on media coverage of athletes with disabilities has been conducted (Brittain, 2010; Yeam & Brooke, 2016; Rees et al. 2017; and Brooke, 2018). Media rarely features para-athletes, and if they do, it has been found to continue to favour a medicalised view of elite para-athletes (Brittain, 2010; Yeam & Brooke, 2016; Rees et al. 2017). This is unfortunate as it is possible that para-athletes challenge habitual expectations from the Empire of the Normal (Coakley, 2009). Further, it was argued that the Paralympics tend to simultaneously empower and disempower, creating what has been termed the Paralympic Paradox (Purdue & Howe, 2012). Those athletes who compete can be seen as benefiting considerably as they have access to artificial limbs. In contrast, there are many who do not have access. Additionally, the 'supercrip' and 'superhuman' narratives have a negative impact on the wider disability community as they cannot live up to the expectations of the public. This has been observed to create an ever-increasing divide within the disabled community at large and this gap is said to be widening the more this mediatised representation of the Paralympics develops (de Silva & Howe, 2012).

The chapter on women who fight was also explored as a socialisation through sport process. Sport's phallocentrism can be seen to impact the way WMMA is viewed currently. In the chapter, it was argued that media attention is unequivocally given to men's sport while women's sport is under-represented and trivialised (Kay, 2003; Kay, & Jeanes, 2008). Despite this, there are undercurrents of change. Polish WMMA star, Jędrzejczyk, also known as Joanna Violence, has received significant media coverage. Moreover, in May 2018, UFC procured new U.S. media rights deals with Disney Direct-to-Consumer and International and ESPN Inc worth $300 million per-year. 42 events on ESPN platforms will be broadcast per-year (Dwornik, 2018). This could be groundbreaking as research into women who fight contends that physical feminism could be a means to 'undoing' the gender order by removing gender stereotypes that women are weaker (McCaughey, 1997; Roth & Basow, 2004; Velija et al. 2013). In contrast, research also demonstrates how patriarchal ideology is actively consented to by some of these women admitting that they participate in martial arts as a form of pleasing the male gaze rather than feminist empowerment (Velija et al. 2013). It was therefore concluded that women who fight might not necessarily find empowerment through physical feminism and that they have to considerably negotiate the presentation of their identities. For real change from the ground up, it was argued that a 'feminist way of being' (Merleau-Ponty, 1962, p. 262) or feminist consciousness (Longwe, as presented in March, Smyth, & Mukhopadhyay, 1999) needs to develop. This is essential, according to Velija et al. (2013), if patriarchal ideology is to be actively deconstructed.

The final chapter was on the well-trodden path of the debate about whether 'sport builds character' (Shields & Bredemeier, 1995; 2001; 2010). On one hand, it appears feasible to see the growth of moral character through sport. Many have researched differing values learned through participation. For example, Nichols et al. (2005) report on research that positive youth development (PYD) was observed in terms of competence, coping and resilience; and Holt et al. (2011b), honesty and respect for self and others. However, as it was pointed out, those who have been labelled 'sport evangelists', a term coined by Giulianotti (2004), often give too much praise to sport and often support their theses with merely anecdotal, even no evidence. Anderson (2013) cites an extract from the *Encyclopedia of Mental Health.* Apart from the psychological wellbeing it proffers, sport is reported to also affect 'other areas of human development, including moral development, social development, and career development' (p. 97). Anderson (20130 points out that no empirical research is cited to substantiate these claims. On the other hand, it is also possible and often argued that sport may implant a taste for aggressive behaviour and egocentric unaltruistic practices (Coakley, 2011; Anderson, 2013). Much research has explored socio-negative impacts of sport participation. In his article, Anderson (2013) discusses how traditional competitive sport leads to several socio-negative impacts on youth such as heteronormativity; hegemonic masculinity; over-adherence to authority; and the normalisation of pain and injury. As a result, a neo-liberal movement represented by i9 has grown. The ideals manifested in i9 sports are in cultural opposition to traditional sports. The consumer-oriented neoliberal approach seems to point towards changes in the traditional structure by developing characteristics such as non-contact, mixed gender activity as well as rotating players and coaches on a regular basis to prevent rivalry. The problem with i9 is that parents pay rendering it exclusive as a middle-class client-based organisation. Thus, any cultural changes do not predominantly impact the lower socio-economic strata and therefore, what we know as modern institutionalised sport.

In conclusion, the topic of sport socialisation comprises a great deal of avenues for study and there are many that remain unexplored. Class, gender, race, physical ability and cultural background are inextricably linked to sport socialisation processes, and their intersection provides a great deal of scope for future studies. Reasons for entering, continuing in, and leaving sport help the researcher to perceive ideologies in society (Bairner, 2007; 2008) and see through their opaqueness and to understand the underlying reasoning and motivations behind such sport participation or lack of it. Sport socialisation also provides a means to investigate the relationships between fundamental concepts in the social sciences such as the debate over whether sport is a mechanism of nature or a result of nurture; and to examine the tensions between structure and agency (Scott & Marshall, 2009).

There are several subjects of interest within this broad field of sport socialisation that could be explored for a future volume of this book. The influence of family culture for socialisation into sport is one avenue; particularly regarding sport as a tool for social mobility. To what extent are children socialised into sport by their parents as a form of trump card for school or college admission? For example, in Confucian Singapore (Marginson, 2011), education is given much greater importance than sport. However, sport can be used as a tool to enter the top schools through the Direct School Admission (DSA) system. Parents are prepared to pay large amounts monthly for coaches for this purpose. It would be interesting to conduct a study on the impacts that this kind of socialisation process has on these children. Are children intrinsically-motivated to participate in their sport or do they consider only instrumental motivations? What are their views regarding their parents' ambitions for them?

More studies can be conducted on eating disorders as a form of socialisation out of sport. There is a strict 'thin' ideal in female sports (Scoffier et al., 2009), particularly in aesthetic sports such as ballet, gymnastics and synchronised swimming. To produce and maintain standards about slenderness, there are official surveillance techniques through coaches' and judges' authority in competitions. This impacts the athletes and they begin to self-discipline (Barker-Ruchti & Tinning, 2010; Johns, 1998). One future study might be on how female athletes exit sport having developed what has now been termed Female Athlete Triad syndrome (FATr), a condition created by the relationship between three independent entities: eating disorders; amenorrhea and osteoporosis (Nattiv et al. 2007). This condition comprises menstrual irregularities and decreased bone mineral density (Nattiv et al. 2007). Finding out how these athletes develop this condition, and finally decide to drop out of sport, would be very valuable. These understandings could help to inform clinicians about how to develop preventative measures early on.

Also, more focus could be given to sporting cultures that are socialised out of the sporting hegemon. Why is it that Chinlone, also known as cane-ball (Aung-Thwin, 2012) and Sepak Takraw, or foot volley ball (Eichberg, 1984), are not global sports like football or tennis? Chinlone (cane-ball) is a Burmese game from the thirteenth century. Up to six athletes form a circle, and without using their hands, ensure the ball remains in the air. There is no direct competition and the sport is deeply associated with Buddhism (Aung-Thwin, 2012). Sepak Takraw's origins are also cooperative and religious (Moser, 2011). In the Malay annals, there are references to the game from the 15th century. With such a longstanding history, a place in the South East Asia Games and several million players and followers, these could be a part of the Olympics. How and why are they socialised out of the global sporting mega-culture?

Further studies in sport and gender are essential. The fast-developing field of WMMA should continue to be analysed, particularly longitudinal studies giving voice to these women who fight as they negotiate the glass ceilings of their gendered embodiment (Channon & Matthews, 2015; Kavoura et al. 2017; Jakubowska et al. 2016). Exploring intersectionality in this field is also essential as differing cultural backgrounds might influence women's sport participation. For example, how are women martial artists in Islamic states treated? How do they negotiate this treatment? Additionally, other sports, such as ultimate frisbee, originally deemed as alternative Birrell, 1988; Theberge & Birrell, 1994), need to be analysed, as they are perhaps shifting from their original meanings of gender equality to the more traditional masculinised forms. Male players in ultimate seem to be increasingly socialising women out of the game (Crocket, 2012).

Studies on master's athletes and how they are empowered through sport is also an ever-evolving and highly interesting study topic. This is important as global ageing is occurring. Generally-speaking, ability to perform decreases with age, particularly in high intensity activities. However, this is not the case for all sports or individuals. Long distance running for example, demonstrates that some runners can produce their best timings in their forties and fifties (Dionigi & O'Flynn, 2007; Tanaka & Seals, 2008). How do these athletes experience their sport? How are they empowered through it? Are they exposed to Moral Panic (Cohen, 2011) and a narrative that renders them as burdensome, needy individuals? If so, how do they negotiate these forces?

The continued development of the Paralympics needs monitoring and voices from the ground level need to be heard, particularly with the reportedly ever-increasing divide within the disabled community (de Silva & Howe, 2012). Further, research on the coverage of athletes with disabilities should continue to demonstrate how the medical model of disability is maintained through the media. Additionally, there is not enough attention paid to those who do not make it to a Paralympic team. Bantjes and Swartz (2017), in *The Conversation (https://theconversation.com/the-odds-are-stacked-against-athletes-from-poor-countries-in-paralympic-sport-70345)*, recently reported how economics play a significant role in socialising athletes out of the Paralympics. They write: 'athletes from low- and middle-income countries – particularly women – are at a distinct disadvantage'. They conclude that 'success is closely related to gross domestic product, team size and country wealth'. Research explicitly looking at these problems as a form of socialisation out of sport is required.

Finally, Fischer (2014) links NFL to the United States military and how both feed off each other. Military activities such as aircraft flyovers and marching soldiers enmeshed in a sea of Stars and Stripes are common to many NFL games. How patriotism through sport is constructed in both spectators and players (Rugg, 2016) is an avenue with a great deal of potential for research. This has become particularly important in recent times with the *take-a-knee movement* started by Kaepernick (Rorke & Copeland, 2017). White supremacists have been vocal about this campaign using the military narrative to view it as disrespectful to the establishment. As a result, Kaepernick has been socialised out of sport (Rorke & Copeland, 2017) and at the time of finishing this book (December 2018), had no NFL contract.

FINAL THOUGHTS

It is this author's belief that sport is and will continue to be an essential global social institution. An extract from Eagleton's *The Meaning of Life: A Very Short Introduction,* began this book with his view that 'it is sport, not religion, which is now the opium of the people' (p. 30). The tensions that exist in our societies are often represented through it. It remains to be seen how and to what extent it might make positive changes in society rather than be used to reinforce discriminatory structures of power. It is hoped that this book has been successful in the pursuit of making explicit some of these phenomena. This is important, as Raymond William's (1977) teaches us, because ideology exists as 'structures of feeling' in our social world. As he states, the hegemonic ideologies 'seem to most of us the pressures and limits of common sense' (p. 110). The book has striven to present and analyse some of the discriminatory practices that are in plain sight. Much of what has been studied in these pages requires attention and transformation; some of it represents possible positive change taking place at the moment.

REFERENCES

Althusser, L. (1971). "Ideology and Ideological State Apparatuses". *Lenin and Philosophy and other Essays.* pp. 121–176.

Anderson, E. (2013). "i9 and the transformation of youth sport". *Journal of Sport and Social Issues, 37*(1), 97-111.

Aung-Thwin, M. (2012). "Towards a national culture: Chinlone and the construction of sport in post-colonial Myanmar". *Sport in Society, 15*(10), 1341-1352.

Bairner, A. (2007). "Back to basics: Class, social theory, and sport". *Sociology of Sport Journal, 24*(1), 20-36.

———. (2008). "Re-appropriating Gramsci: Marxism, hegemony and sport". In *Marxism, cultural studies and sport* (pp. 229-246). Routledge.

Bantjes, J., & Swartz. L. (2017). The odds are stacked against athletes from poor countries in paralympic sport. *The Conversation.* Retrieved December 2018 from *https://theconversation.com/the-odds-are-stacked-against-athletes-from-poor-countries-in-paralympic-sport-70345.*

Barker-Ruchti, N., & Tinning, R. (2010). Foucault in leotards: Corporeal discipline in women's artistic gymnastics. *Sociology of Sport Journal, 27*(3), 229-250.

Beamon, K, K. (2010) "Are Sports Overemphasized in the Socialization Process of African American Males? A Qualitative Analysis of Former Collegiate Athletes' Perception of Sport Socialization". *Journal of Black Studies, 41(2)*, 281–300.

Beamon, K. K., & Bell, P. A. (2006). Academics versus athletics: An examination of the effects of background and socialization on African American male student athletes. Social Science Journal, 43(3), 393-403.

Beamon, K. K., & Bell, P. A. (2011). A dream deferred: Narratives of African American male former collegiate athletes' transition out of sports and into the occupational sector. Journal for the Study of Sports and Athletes in Education, 5(1), 29-44.

Beedie, P., & Craig, P. (Eds.). (2010). *Sport sociology*. London: Learning Matters.

Birrell, S. J. (1988). "Discourses on the gender/sport relationship: from women in sport to gender relations". *Exercise and sport sciences reviews*, *16*, 459-502.

———. (2000). "Feminist theories for sport". In *Handbook of Sports Studies*. In J. Coakley and E. Dunning. (Eds). London: Sage Publications. (pp. 61-76).

Bourdieu, P. (1986). "The forms of capital". In J. Richardson (Ed.) *Handbook of Theory and Research for the Sociology of Education*, New York, Greenwood, 241-258.

Brooke, M. (2015). "Fongzi, dragons and corporate culture: An analysis of corporate dragon-boat paddlers' motivations". *Asia Pacific Journal of Sport and Social Science*, 4*(2)*, 1-12.

Brooke, M. (2018). The Singaporean Paralympics and Its Media Portrayal: Real Sport? Men-Only? *Communication & Sport*, 6(5), 1-20. DOI: 2167479518784278.

Channon, A., & Matthews, C. R. (2015). "It is what it is: Masculinity, homosexuality, and inclusive discourse in mixed martial arts". *Journal of homosexuality*, *62*(7), 936-956.

Coakley, J. J. (2009). *Sports in Society: Issues and Controversies*. Edition, 10, McGraw-Hill Education.

———. (2011). "Youth sports: What counts as positive development?". *Journal of sport and social issues*, *35*(3), 306-324.

Cohen, S. (2011). *Folk devils and moral panics*. Routledge. UK.

Connell, R. (1987). *Gender and Power: Society, the Person, and Sexual Politics*. Stanford University Press. US.

Crocket, H. (2013). "This is men's ultimate:(Re) creating multiple masculinities in elite open Ultimate Frisbee". *International Review for the Sociology of Sport*, 48(3), 318-333.

Delaney, T., & Madigan, T. (2015). *The sociology of sports: An introduction*. North Carolina: McFarland.

Dionigi, R., & O'Flynn, G. (2007). "Performance discourses and old age: What does it mean to be an older athlete?" *Sociology of sport journal*, 24(4), 359-377.

Dwornik, A. (2018). The Walt Disney Company's Direct to Consumer and International Segment and ESPN Reach Groundbreaking Agreement with UFC for Media Rights & Distribution. *ESPN Media Zone*, https://espnmediazone.com/us/press-releases/2018/05/the-walt-disney-companys-direct-to-consumer-and-international-segment-and-espn-reach-groundbreaking-agreement-with-ufc-for-media-rights-distribution/

Eagleton, T. (2007). *The meaning of life*. Oxford University Press. Oxford.

Edwards, H. (2000). "Crisis of Black athletes on the eve of the 21st century". *Society, 37*, 9–13.

Eichberg, H. (1984). "Olympic sport-Neocolonization and alternatives". *International review for the sociology of sport*, *19*(1), 97-106.

Fischer, M. (2014). "Commerating 9/11 NFL-Style: Insights into America's Culture of Militarism". *Journal of Sports and Social Issues, 38*(3), 199-221.

Foddy, B., & Savulescu, J. (2011). "Time to re-evaluate gender segregation in athletics?" *Br J Sports Med*, *45*(15), 1184-1188.

Giulianotti, R. (2004). *Sport and modern social theorists*. Springer. UK.

Gramsci, A. (1971). *Selections from the Prison Notebooks of Antonio Gramsci*. Ed. and Transl. by Quintin Hoare and Geoffrey Nowell Smith. New York: International Publishers.

Hill, D. (2010). "A critical mass of corruption: why some football leagues have more match-fixing than others". *International Journal of Sports Marketing and Sponsorship*, *11*(3), 38-52.

Hoberman, J. M. (2001). *Mortal engines: The science of performance and the dehumanization of sport*. Blackburn Press.

Holt, N. L., & Neely, K. C. (2011b). "Positive youth development through sport: A review". *Revista iberoamericana de psicología del ejercicio y el deporte*, *6*(2).

Hong, F. (2004). "Innocence Lost: Child Athletes in China". *Sport in Society*, *7*(3), 338-354

Hong, F., Wu P. & Xiong H. (2005). "Beijing Ambitions: An Analysis of the Chinese Elite Sports System and its Olympic Strategy for the 2008 Olympic Games". *The International Journal of the History of Sport*, *22*(4), 510-529.

Human Rights Watch (2016). Saudi Arabia: Women Are "Changing the Game". *Human Rights Watch*. Retrieved from https://www.hrw.org/news/2016/08/04/saudi-arabia-women-are-changing-game

Jakubowska, H., Channon, A., & Matthews, C. R. (2016). "Gender, media, and mixed martial arts in Poland: The case of Joanna Jędrzejczyk". *Journal of Sport and Social Issues*, *40*(5), 410-431.

Johns, D.P. (1998) 'Fasting and Feasting: Paradoxes of the Sport Ethic', *Sociology of Sport Journal* 15: 41-63.

Kavoura, A., Kokkonen, M., Chroni, S. & Ryba, T. V. (2017). "Some women are born fighters: Discursive constructions of a Fighter's identity by female Finnish judo athletes". *Sex Roles*, 1-14.

Kay, T. (2003). "Sport and gender". *Sport and society: A student introduction,* 89-104.

Kay, T., & Jeanes, R. (2008). "Women, sport and gender inequity". *Sport and society*: *A student introduction,* 2, 130-154.

Kay, J., & Laberge, S. (2002). "The 'new' corporate habitus in adventure racing". *International Review for the Sociology of Sport*. 37*(1),* 17–36.

Lane, S., & Jackson, E. (2017). "Female gamers face sexism and bullying in e-sports competitions", *ABC*. Retrieved from http://www.abc.net.au/radio/programs/am/female-gamers-face-sexism-and-bullying-in-e-sports/8516486

Leonard, W. (1998). *A Sociological Perspective of Sport* (5th edition), Boston: Allyn and Bacon.

Loebenberg, A. (2018). "What is the state of play?" *International Journal of Play*, 1-5.

Lupton, D. (2014, December). "Self-tracking cultures: towards a sociology of personal informatics". In *Proceedings of the 26th Australian Computer-Human Interaction Conference on Designing Futures: The Future of Design* (pp. 77-86). ACM.

Lupton, D. (2016). *The quantified self.* Polity: Cambridge.

March, C., Smyth, I. A., & Mukhopadhyay, M. (1999). *A guide to gender-analysis frameworks*. Oxfam: UK.

Marginson, S. (2011). Higher education in east Asia and Singapore: Rise of the confucian model. *Higher Education*, *61*(5), 587-611.

McCaughey, M. (1997). *Real knockouts: The physical feminism of women's self-defense*. NYU Press.

Messner, M. A. (1988). Sports and male domination: The female athlete as contested ideological terrain. *Sociology of Sport Journal*, 5, 197–211.

Messner, M. A. (2002). *Taking the field: Women, men, and sports*. U of Minnesota Press. US.

Moser, S. (2011). "Constructing cultural heritage". *International Institute for Asian Studies Newsletter*, *57*, 30-31.

Nattiv, A., Loucks, A. B., Manore, M. M., Sanborn, C. F., Sundgot-Borgen, J., & Warren, M. P. (2007). "The female athlete triad special communications: position stand". *Med Sci Sports Exerc*, *39*(10), 1867-82.

Nichols, G., Taylor, P., James, M., Holmes, K., King, L., & Garrett, R. (2005). "Pressures on the UK voluntary sport sector". *Voluntas: International Journal of Voluntary and Nonprofit Organizations*, *16*(1), 33-50.

Orlick, T. D. (1974). Sport Participation-A process of shaping behavior. *Human Factors: The Journal of the Human Factors and Ergonomics Society*, *16*(5), 558-561.

Purdue, D. E. J., & Howe, P. D. (2012). "See the sport, not the disability: exploring the Paralympic paradox". *Qualitative research in sport, exercise and health*, *4*(2), 189-205.

Rees, L., Robinson, P., & Shields, N. (2017). Media portrayal of elite athletes with disability–a systematic review. *Disability and rehabilitation*, 1-8.

Rorke, T., & Copeland, A. (2017). "Athletic disobedience: providing a context for analysis of Colin Kaepernick's protest". *FairPlay, Revista de Filosofia, Ética y Derecho del Deporte*, (10), 83-107.

Roth, A., & Basow, S. A. (2004). "Femininity, sports, and feminism: Developing a theory of physical liberation". *Journal of Sport and Social Issues, 28*(3), 245-265.

Rugg, A. (2016). "America's game: The NFL's 'Salute to Service' campaign, the diffused military presence, and corporate social responsibility". *Popular Communication the International Journal of Media and Culture, 14*(1), 21-29.

Savulescu, J. (2015). "Why we should legalise performance-enhancing drugs in sport1". *Routledge Handbook of Drugs and Sport*, pp. 350-376.

Scoffier, S., Maïano, C., & d'Arripe-Longueville, F. (2010;2009;). The effects of social relationships and acceptance on disturbed eating attitudes in elite adolescent female athletes: The mediating role of physical self-perceptions. *The International Journal of Eating Disorders, 43*(1), 65-71.

Scott, J., & Marshall, G. (Eds.). (2009). *A dictionary of sociology*. Oxford University Press, USA.

Shields, D. L. L., & Bredemeier, B. J. L. (1995). *Character development and physical activity*. Human Kinetics Publishers.

———. (2001). "Moral development and behavior in sport". *Handbook of sport psychology*, *2*, 585-603.

———. (2010). "Competition: Was Kohn, right?" *Phi Delta Kappan, 91*(5), 62-67.

Silva, C. F. & Howe, P. D. (2012). "The (in) validity of supercrip representation of Paralympian athletes". *Journal of Sport and Social Issues, 36*(2), 174-194.

Sullivan, C. F. (2011). "Gender VErification and Gender Policies in Elite Sport: Eligibility and Fair Play". *Journal of Sport and Social Issues*, 35, (4), 400-419.

Tanaka, H., & Seals, D. R. (2008). "Endurance exercise performance in master's athletes: age-associated changes and underlying physiological mechanisms". *The Journal of physiology*, *586*(1), 55-63.

Taylor, T. L. (2012). *Raising the Stakes: E-sports and the Professionalization of Computer Gaming*. MIT Press.

Theberge, N., & Birrell, S. (1994). "The sociological study of women and sport". *Women and sport: Interdisciplinary perspectives*, 323-330.

Velija, P., Mierzwinski, M., & Fortune, L. (2013). "It made me feel powerful: women's gendered embodiment and physical empowerment in the martial arts". *Leisure studies, 32*(5), 524-541.

Walseth, K. (2006). "Young Muslim women and sport: The impact of identity work". *Leisure studies, 25*(1), 75-94.

Williams, R. (1977). *Marxism and Literature*, Oxford: Oxford University Press, UK.

Lightning Source UK Ltd.
Milton Keynes UK
UKHW052325010319
338232UK00005B/23/P